Benard's Vision

THE QUEST OF A KENYAN PASTOR

BETH ANN MORGAN

D1417869

AMPELOS PRESS
DREXEL HILL, PA

Cover design by Christine Quier

Cover photo Copyright © David Logan 2007
All rights reserved.
flickr.com/photos/davidloganphotography

Back cover photo by Sarah Bothwell

Inside design and editing by Marlene Bagnull

Map by Bob Lockwood, Full Armour Studios

Inside photos by Sarah Bothwell, Beth Ann Morgan, Don C. Perrin II, Dr. Scott Rice, and Greg Wollenhaupt

ISBN 978-0-9821653-0-0

Published by Ampelos Press (www.writehisanswer.com) for
Dublin Bible Church
427 Airport Road
Dublin, GA 31021

Printed in the United States of America.

This book is dedicated with love to

Laura Beth Wollenhaupt,

the courageous young woman who
dared to do more to impact eternity
in her twenty years on earth
than most people hope to do in a lifetime.

October 22, 1983 – August 14, 2004

May we all live with her passion to love others in Jesus' name.

Acknowledgments

Many thanks to:

Dr. George W. Murray and Columbia International University (CIU).

2004 Team from CIU – Laura Wollenhaupt, Chris Matthews, and Genevieve Ferrin.

2004 Team from Trinity Baptist Church, Casey, South Carolina – Sean Roddy (Team Leader), Ben Byxbe, Sarah Bothwell, Julianne Wolfe, Natasha Gordon, Mark Canada, and Will Harrison.

2005 Team from CIU – Ben Byxbe (Team Leader), Luke Roberts, Nathan Forrest, Genevieve Ferrin, Alicia Hardy, Noel Marquard, and Jodi Sjerven.

2005 Team from Faith Evangelical Free Church, Allentown, PA – Greg Wollenhaupt (Team Leader), Dr. Scott Rice (Medical Team Leader), Sue Wollenhaupt, Amy Wollenhaupt Perez, Lori Dauscher, Michelle Flores, Donna Frank, Krystal Kostura, Patricia Liever, Lo Miles, Beth Ann Morgan, Don C. Perrin II, Jennifer Reidy, Danielle Saul, Angie Smith, and Josh Whalen.

All of these teams raised financial donations, medical supplies, and prayer support from numerous businesses, churches, family members, individuals, and organizations including Lehigh Valley Hospital and Health Network and Gateway Baptist Church of Charlotte, NC.

Christian T. Morgan, Don C. Perrin II, Diane Hernandez, Ashley Morgan, Kathy Tyers, the Lehigh Valley Christian Writers Group, Judy Perrin, Krissie Perrin, Alan Allegra, Christine Quier, and Bob and Beki Lockwood for their editorial input, support, and encouragement.

My personal prayer team consisting of Jenny and Krissie Perrin, Betty Tirrado, Helen Hwang, Christine Quier, and Kimberly Kuschel.

Chris Matthews, Teri Miles, Ben Byxbe, and Alicia Hardy for enduring extensive interviews.

Cec Murphey for his generous support in promoting Benard's Vision and Carmen Leal for connecting him to the project.

Christine Quier (cover design and layout), David Logan (front cover photo), Sarah Bothwell (back cover photo), and Bob Lockwood (map) for their excellent work.

Marlene Bagnull for catching the vision and seeing it through every step of the way.

Special thanks for your wise counsel and support to Colby Kinser and Dublin Bible Church, Sarah Bothwell, Brian and Yvonne Bleam, Dr. Robert M. and Karen Griffin Jr., Michelle Leight, Steve McLeod, Don C. Perrin II, and Dr. Scott Rice.

Greg and Sue Wollenhaupt for freely sharing Laura's story.

Benard and Pamela Ondiek for willingly sharing their story.

Our gracious Heavenly Father who has masterfully woven all of these lives together to reveal His great love for the men and women, boys and girls, of Kenya.

*Where there is no vision
the people perish.*

Proverbs 29:18 (KJV)

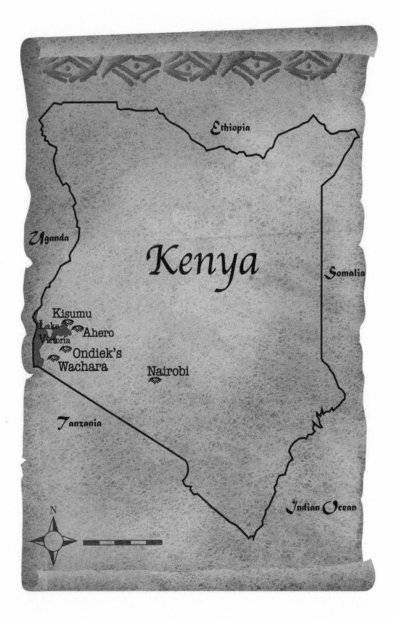

Contents

Foreword

When I read the inspiring story of Benard and Pamela Ondiek, and how, in God's providence, their lives intersected with Laura Wollenhaupt, two words come immediately to mind: simple and short. Let me explain.

Benard and Pamela are simple people. Theirs is not a life of complicated pretense, but of simple faith and integrity. What you see is what you get. Speaking of the virtues of simplicity, best-selling author Robert J. Morgan puts it this way in *Simple* (Nashville: Randall House Publications, 2006):

> If anyone should be an expert in simplicity, it's the Christian. It's not that we're simple-*minded*; we deal with the deepest truths under heaven. But we are simple of heart and habit. And while our beliefs are deep enough to challenge the world's greatest thinkers, they're plain enough for children to understand.

The Ondieks are simple of heart and habit. But "simple" doesn't mean "easy." On the contrary, Benard and Pamela's life has often been very difficult. Nor does "simple" mean "dull," as you will find out by reading the colorful and exciting pages of this book. Their adventures of simple faith and selfless sacrifice in Kenya are truly inspiring.

Laura Wollenhaupt's life was very short, just twenty years here on this earth. And her public ministry as a young adult was even shorter. To me, Laura was a modern flesh-and-blood example of the humility and prophetic passion of John the Baptizer. Because John was so humble, Jesus called him great, and though his public ministry was less than a year long, its impact continues to shake us all. That was Laura. I remember well when she boldly asked for a personal appointment with me, the President of the university she was attending. In that one-hour conversation she passionately poured out her heart of vision for the people of Kenya. In this book you will catch that others-centered vision and passion.

What I say above is not written just because I have read *Benard's Vision*; it is written because I, personally, have known the people this book is talking about. I've seen them up close. They're the real deal. May God help each of us to live lives of simple obedient faith, like Benard, Pamela, and Laura, regardless of how long or short our time on earth may be.

George W. Murray, President
Columbia International University

Part One

Chosen

*"For many are called,
but few are chosen."*

Matthew 22:14

Chapter One

Child of Promise

WACHARA, KENYA ~ DECEMBER 8, 1959

*T*he joyous anticipation of a new life clashed with the midwife's desperate news. "Your wife is having trouble," she said as she avoided his eyes. She appeared frightened and did little to mask it. "Her pain is great, and her labor is difficult."

Papa Julu, father of seven, stared at the floor and resumed his pacing. As his bare feet shuffled across the cool earthen floor, fingers of fear threatened to reach in and strangle his heart. Maybe he should fetch the witch-man. A scream pierced the darkness, sickening him.

The midwife glanced over her shoulder and then grabbed a pile of clean rags. "I must go." She ran into the next room, calling words of comfort ahead of her.

Left alone in the living area of the tiny dwelling, Papa Julu stood and surveyed the homemade table and chairs, remembering the joy on his wife's face the day he had made them. What would he do if she . . . He couldn't lose her, not now. She moaned, the sound sending chills down his spine. He looked up as the midwife entered the room carrying a tiny baby wrapped in a clean shirt.

"Your son." She thrust the small bundle forward, allowing herself a small smile.

"I will call him Benard. Benard Okumu Ondiek." Papa took his son and held him close, tears clouding his vision. He dreaded asking the awful question. "My wife?"

"She is very sick and can have no more children."

"Benard, do you know the answer?" Thirty-five pairs of brown eyes stared at him while the teacher brushed chalk dust from her dark hands.

"I believe the answer is 26," he said in his booming baritone.

Teacher closed her eyes and gave a slight nod in his direction. "Well done, Benard. Well done."

He breathed a sigh of relief. As the only ten-year-old in a room full of five- and six-year-olds, Benard felt self-conscious, not to mention gigantic. All of the children loved him and were happy when he had joined their class. Even though Papa came to get him four times during the school day to care for Mama, Benard soaked up every figure, chart, and book his mind could hold.

He loved school. Maybe someday he would go to college.

Footsteps filled the back of the small classroom as the headmaster of the school entered with Benard's stone-faced father trailing behind. Neither looked at Benard. His heart began to pound.

Teacher came forward and spoke with the two men, nodding and glancing occasionally at Benard. She appeared concerned, and he grew all the more nervous. After a few minutes, she sighed, her shoulders slumping.

"Benard, gather your things. You will not come back to school after today."

Tears threatened to fall as he stood with his small writing tablet. He did not look at Papa but turned to wave at the students.

"Goodbye, friends. Do well for Teacher. I have to take care of Mama." Benard turned to face Teacher. "Thank you for all you have taught me. I will not forget anything."

She said nothing, but Benard saw her wipe away a tear.

"Hurry, Benard! Hurry!" his oldest brother urged carrying the other side of their sibling's feverish body that swayed like a half-empty sack of wheat, seeming more like a corpse than the wide-eyed smiling boy Benard loved. "The hospital cannot be much farther."

Benard could not respond. His eleven-year-old legs struggled to keep pace with his brother's quick strides over the uneven dung road. Almost there, almost there. He had to keep moving. His brother's life depended on it. As drops of sweat beaded along his forehead and rolled down his face, he felt tiny pricks of mosquitoes feasting upon his arms and legs. But he must forget the mosquitoes. Forget the hunger pangs and side stickers.

Forget himself.

One glance at his brother's clammy face and glassy eyes in the moonlight stirred hidden anger. Benard had seen too much death in his young life, and now, it had come to claim one of his own. Death lurked everywhere, hiding behind many names but yielding the same devastation, darkness, and despair.

People died like chickens, and nobody cared.

Days later, Benard watched as weeping men lowered his brother into the ground. The witch-man came and sang incantations over the grave, eerily dancing and chanting around the freshly dug earth. Spirals of smoke from fire and incense burned Benard's nostrils, sickening him. He slipped away unnoticed into the tall grassy plain.

Benard liked feeling the tall grass crunch under his feet. His sister's warning about a lioness roaming the village flashed through his mind, but he could not resist the temptation to escape to his favorite place. He loved melting into the scenery of his native Kenyan homeland and pretending that he was far away. Away from the cooking, cleaning, and caretaking responsibilities that had fallen upon him the night of his birth.

Kenyan tradition dictated that the youngest child in each family should care for his parents until they died if they became ill or unable to support themselves. Because Benard's mother had been seriously ill and disabled since delivering him, Benard had grown up taking over her duties and caring for her physical needs. The head of the house was not expected to do this as long as children lived in the home.

Benard sighed, not wanting to leave his haven in the grass but knowing Mama would soon worry about him. As he drew near, he heard his sister's soprano Luo.

"I warned him about the lioness, Mama," she said. "He'd better be back soon."

He could now see her fold her arms across her chest. When his gaze swept to Mama, he gasped. Mama looked as if she had walked a hundred miles. How must she feel, he wondered, after burying a son today? He shuddered.

"Benard will come, child." Mama stared at nothing. "Yes, he will come."

Benard shuffled forward, his hands in his pockets. "I'm back, Mama."

"You went to the plain, didn't you, Benard?"

He nodded, eyes averted.

Mama shooed her daughter into the house. Once she was gone, Mama placed a hand on his arm. "Benard, I must rest now," she said, draping her bony arms around his neck.

"Yes, Mama." He gently lifted her frail body and carried her into the bedroom, laying her on the thin mattress. Her worn sandals unfastened easily as Benard took them from her feet. "Do you need anything, Mama?" he asked as he placed a hand on her warm cheek.

"No, thank you, my son."

"Rest, Mama. I will come back with your supper." He slipped away.

Hours later, Benard sat at her side spooning a steamy stew to her lips. Her body trembled as she strained forward, her lips slowly parting. Sweet Mama. After she swallowed a sip, she sank back with a thud. His thoughts began to wander when the quivering of her voice startled him.

"You never complain about taking care of me, Bernard," she said as she squirmed to find a more comfortable position. "You are such a bright boy. You must go back to school—"

"Hush, Mama. You need to rest." He took a rag and wiped her mouth, making sure that all traces of the stew were rubbed away. How well she knew him. He would give anything to be back in school every day, to be with the other kids learning new and exciting things. Somehow, he had managed to complete standards one and two while taking care of Mama, but keeping up with both had become too difficult. He sighed as he remembered the day Papa had come to school and Teacher had told him he would not be returning.

Going to school like a regular kid was only a dream.

"Perhaps Papa will let you return to school."

Why was she thinking about this today, the day of his brother's funeral? She made no sense.

"No, Mama." Blinking hard, Benard shook his head and dropped the spoon in the dish. "I am your youngest child, and our custom says your care is my duty. Actually, I consider it my honor to care for you, Mama." He gazed tenderly at her, but she had looked away.

"You must go, Benard." She fixed her eyes on something faraway, something unseen. "Yes, Benard, you must go." Her tears flowed freely as she waved her hand around the room. "There is nothing for you here."

"But if I leave, who will look after you? How will—"

She feebly raised a palm. "Leave me. I must mourn my son."

"Yes, Mama." He stooped to kiss her forehead. "Good night."

Pastor Benard's
homestead in
Wachara, Kenya

Pastor Benard and Papa

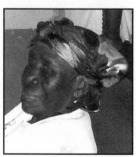

Mama

The barn

Chapter Two

Door to the Future

ONE MONTH LATER

A warm Kenyan breeze brushed the beautiful face of the lone matatu patron. Her driver glanced in the rearview mirror occasionally, seemingly curious about her mission. She had maintained a crisp yet polite conversation with him for the first fifty miles, and now she rode in silence.

She pictured her brother working at home while most other children his age soaked in facts and figures at school. Shifting in her seat, she stared out the window but never saw the breathtaking countryside. *Poor Benard. He never complains, but he must long to join his friends and learn about the world.*

Alice clenched her fists and felt heat flushing her face as she thought of her parents. How could they allow him to sacrifice so much? But then her hands relaxed as love washed over her. Papa had the enormous responsibility of providing for his large brood without a helpful wife, and even though several of her siblings had married or moved away, Papa still kept Benard home to cook, clean, and look after Mama.

Papa is a good man, but it is time. Alice had decided that Benard must come with her. He would have no life unless she took him away from that place. The familiar one-half acre came into view, complete with a modest-sized brick dwelling and several chickens and goats grazing out front. She tried to appear more confident than she felt. *Please, Papa, let Benard go.*

The matatu came to a halt.

"Benard!" she called.

He hurried toward her and engulfed her in a huge hug as the driver remained inside the running passenger van.

"Tell your driver to come in. I'll feed you lunch."

"Go get your things, Benard. We are leaving," his sister ordered him.

Confusion spread across Benard's face. He stepped aside as she marched through the rickety door frame to speak with their parents. Papa and Mama looked up from the table in surprise. Their daughter stooped to hug them and took a deep breath. As gently as she could, she broke it to them.

"I have come to take Benard to live with me in Lucinda Highland to get an education."

Mama's eyes filled with tears, and Papa stared at the floor. Benard said nothing, seeming to wrestle with excitement and grief all at once. Mama rallied first, speaking softly to Papa.

"Please let Benard go with her. He needs an education, and he has given up so much already."

Silence filled the room. Benard hovered in the doorway with downcast eyes. Compassion for him filled Alice's heart as she stood next to the wobbly table, waiting.

"I know this is sudden, Papa," she said, "but it is best for Benard's future."

Time crawled by. Finally, Papa stood and shuffled to the door to face Benard. "You may go. I want you to get an education."

Benard hugged his father and then reached for his mother. He lingered in her embrace, breathing in the scent of her.

"You have worked hard, my son. I am so proud of you," Mama said as she pressed a weary hand against his chest and smiled wide.

Benard broke into his patented grin. After stroking Mama's cheek, he turned to his elated sister. "I am ready now."

Four Years Later

Shoppers carrying baskets of grain and fish on their heads fanned out in clusters of two or three ahead of Benard and his sister on the road out of the village. Alice had insisted on accompanying him to the edge of Lucinda Highland by Lake Victoria. A bicyclist rang his bell at them. The siblings exchanged a glance as they exited the busy marketplace.

"You have done well during your stay with me, Benard," Alice complimented. "Give Mama and Papa my love."

Benard smiled at her, grateful that she had come and taken him out of Wachara five years ago to complete standards three through six. Lately, thoughts of their mother had consumed Benard, and Alice had noticed. Both of them had known it was time for his return to Wachara.

"Thank you for all you have done for me, Alice," he said. "Thank you for bringing me here."

They embraced, and Benard set off barefoot down the dusty road. Sister had sent a small bag of chapati flat bread and bananas with him, fuel for the five-day journey stretching before him. He had never walked this far before, but he would do it.

While he plodded silently along, Benard realized how much he had enjoyed learning and reading unhindered by the responsibility of caring for his ailing mother. He hungered for more education and yet yearned for his mother. His footsteps quickened as the sun bore down across the African plain. Soon he would be home.

"Welcome home, Benard!" Mama held her arms out. He rushed to embrace her.

"Mama! How are you?" He studied her new wrinkles and whitening hair. "How are you feeling?"

She waved his question aside. "I'm the same, Benard. Nothing's changed. But please, I want to hear all about school and about Alice."

Benard obliged until Papa came home with the news that Benard would complete standards seven and eight while living with a cousin near the Tanzania border. Benard's face fell. Home a few hours only to leave again.

He hated leaving his mother, but Benard honored his father and moved one month later. After completing standard seven and half of eight, Benard decided to run away and returned to Wachara, determined to take care of his mother.

Benard strolled through his favorite patch of tall grass far enough from the house to feel "away" and yet close enough to hear if Mama called. He had to think. Although he had been barely managing to keep up with his household duties while going to school, he would be finished with standard eight shortly. Then what?

The Kenyan educational system provided all citizens free access to standards one through eight, but families were responsible for secondary school. Most parents could not afford the uniforms, books, and the time away from supporting the family required for older children to go to school, so many of Benard's bright, capable friends quit after standard eight to become fishermen, farmers, and parents at the age of thirteen or fourteen.

He hunkered down on a small patch of dirt. Grasping a stalk of grass he yanked it out of the earth, glad to busy his hands. The coarse, stringy plant brushed his palms as he stripped the feathery head and rolled it between his fingers. He bent the reed in half and tossed it aside.

At eighteen, Benard had already fallen well behind the other children. All of his brothers and sisters had finished school and married. He alone remained with his parents. Mama continued to do poorly. The nasty, bloody rash covered her body and tortured her daily, and he hated thinking about leaving her again. But he must. He inhaled deeply, slowly nodding. Yes, he must continue with school. He rose and looked toward the family homestead, nodding again.

He must do something about his life.

"Papa, you wanted to talk with me about my education?"

Papa glanced up from whittling a table leg and motioned for his son to sit next to him.

Benard eyed the main room of their humble living quarters. Pale green paint coated the four concrete walls, each decorated with framed photographs of famous politicians and educated men. The familiar setting did little to calm his pounding heart as he sat down next to Papa.

What would Papa say? Benard knew his parents did not have the money to pay tuition.

"Benard, you have done well in school." Papa paused. "A new high school will open this term."

Benard straightened, his eyes widening. A new school! Here was his chance.

"The school is far away," Papa continued. "Can you walk six hours every day?"

Benard could not answer. His throat thickened, and beads of sweat broke out across his forehead. School! A secondary school!

"I have talked to the headmaster of the school about you, and he admitted you immediately because of your good past." Papa's strong gaze bore into Benard. "My son, I will do my best. I will sell all of my land to take you to school. I will even become a watchman for anybody for you to go to school."

Breathing deeply and trying to withhold his tears, Benard made his vow. "Papa, I will not disappoint you."

A truck stuck in the mud, a common occurrence after a heavy rain. The roads are made of dung and are very difficult to travel.

Chapter Three

Life of Surrender

The sky was bluer than any he had ever seen. Benard whistled as he walked down the dusty brown trail. A weathered shirt and baggy trousers clung to his moist body, but he didn't mind. He enjoyed the hot sun beating down on his wiry frame mile after mile, making him feel alive and refreshed after his first day of secondary school.

When he had stopped for water a while back, three bloody spots on his cracked feet had warned him to stop walking, but he had ignored them. Nothing was going to stop him from going to school. Nothing. He wanted to learn more than anything.

Papa had become a watchman by night so that he could care for Benard's mother by day. Other relatives also contributed a little money, and Benard hoped that within four years, he would finish the distinguished Form Four.

A small red book fell from his weary arms, and he rushed to retrieve it from the road. After picking it up, he inspected it like Papa did paper money. Benard sighed and put the book atop the stack he carried. He must be more careful and learn how to travel home without a bag since there was no money to buy one.

Hearing the roar of his empty stomach, Benard quickened his pace. His legs quivered in protest, his muscles aching from the many miles they had already endured. He wiped his brow with the upper part of his shirtsleeve and squinted. *Not much longer, Benard,* he said to himself. *You must keep going. You must do this thing.*

He forced his mind to positive thoughts. At least the headmaster said that Benard didn't have to wear a uniform. All of the boys at school loathed their confining shirts and pants, as well as shoes. Many preferred to go barefoot like Benard, and he felt sorry for them as he enjoyed the simple pleasures his humble circumstances allowed.

Smells of chapati bread and lentil stew filled his nostrils. A new vigor flooded his veins, and all pain left him as his pace quickened. Soon he would be home and could help serve the simple meal, after which he would do chores and homework. Then he would go to bed, and it would be morning.

What a wonderful thing it was to go to school!

Like a nightmare, Benard found himself once again on the road to the hospital in the dead of night. Fear propelled Benard and his brother as they rushed their youngest sister down the long dung road to the hospital. She had fallen sick during a holiday celebration at their parents' home, and now the lively girl lay limp on the woven mat. The black night swallowed the trio, whispering death and despair into their souls.

Not again, Benard's heart cried as his mind groped to understand, but reason escaped him. He must hurry. Glancing down at his sister, he saw her eyes wide open. Too wide, too open. He shouted an alarm to his brother.

"Stop!" When his brother glared at him and refused to slow his step, Benard jutted his chin toward their sister. "Look!"

His brother took in her glazed, open eyes and halted. They stared at her corpse in shock not wanting to believe she had left them. Lowering her body to the ground, they collapsed weeping beside her.

Anger swept over Benard like a brush fire. They'd had only twenty miles left! *Oh, why, why had she left them?* His anger burned hot. Another sibling, dead. Dead. His brother rose and motioned for Benard to pick up their sister. Their burden seemed heavier now, and they grunted as they hefted her weight into the air.

As they headed home, Benard's mind raced through the maze of grief not only for his family but also for his people. Such great suffering. Would this be his fate, to die in the middle of the night while traveling in agony to the hospital that was too far away to help? He grimaced.

What about Mama? Papa? Everyone I love? The problem of unclean water, disease, food shortage, and inadequate medical care touched everyone he knew, leaving many of his friends without parents or relatives to care for them.

The men of Wachara that could do physical labor often supported their families by daily riding a bicycle to Lake Victoria. There, they would fish and sell their catch at the local market. After earning all they could, they would wearily climb on their bikes and pedal back to the village.

Men of the village died young due to hard work and lack of food. Without education, Benard would be forced to follow such a path as this—one that would ultimately lead to a premature death. Women, too, died young. They hauled heavy pails of water for washing, cleaning, cooking, and bathing. They carried bundles of grain and food and laundry on their heads, putting stress on their necks, backs, and legs. Between hard labor and malnutrition, families all around Benard struggled endlessly to maintain health and home.

Was there no end to the hunger, to the struggling? To the death?

"Stop dreaming and concentrate," his brother snapped when his sister's stiff form nearly rolled off the mat.

Benard lifted his side higher, resolving to do his part in this last act of love for his sister. As he shifted her weight, cold taut skin brushed his hand, and he jumped, once again thrust into the harsh reality of the night. He must get more education and get a job. Then, he would take Mama to the best doctor. He stole a glance at his sister.

Death was the enemy.

"Benard, Benard, did you hear?"

Benard looked up from his history text. "Hear what?"

His classmate's eyes sparkled as he clasped his hands in front of him. "A member of Parliament plans to attend the music competition next week!" The student whirled in delight and ran to share his tasty morsel with a trio of students entering the room.

Benard froze, thankful his friend had gone. *If only he knew,* Benard thought. He pretended to focus on his studies, but he could barely contain his anxiety.

His thoughts wandered to the rumpled scrap of paper he had hidden between pages 37 and 38 of his history book. The music teacher had informed him last week of the politician's visit and had asked Benard to write a song in his honor.

Happily, Benard complied. The words flowed out of an eager heart as he realized he would get to sing for the coming guest. He finished and ran into the main living quarters of his home to show his parents his work. Visiting relatives and friends packed the small room, and Benard spotted his mother in a corner.

"Mama, I want to show you the song I have written for the Member of Parliament who is coming to the music competition in two weeks."

She frowned and pulled her shawl tightly about her. Everyone in the room fell quiet and exchanged angry glances. Benard searched the stony faces for answers but none came. The stillness that followed seemed to make dragonflies dance in his stomach.

Mama later informed him that the entire Wachara clan disapproved of his participation in the event. The clan held to traditional Seventh-day Adventist beliefs and refused to endorse any type of secular music, including the songs students would sing at the competition. Benard had not understood how the lyrics he had written interfered with his religion and had wanted to perform with the other students. Even now, he wrestled with his loyalty to the clan and his desire to honor the important guest.

"Benard." His history teacher nodded toward the doorway where the music teacher stood beside an unfamiliar man in a suit.

"They wish to speak with you."

Benard had already told his teacher that he would not be able to perform. After closing his book, he rose and met the pair in the hallway, taking comfort in his music teacher's encouraging smile. He introduced the stranger with him as the organizer of the music competition, and Benard shook his hand in wonder.

"It is nice to meet you, sir. I'm sorry I cannot sing with the other students at the event." Benard frowned and looked down.

The music teacher cleared his throat as his companion stepped closer to Benard and spoke.

"Young man, your teacher told me that the song you have written honoring the Member of Parliament is very good, and we believe you should be the one to sing it to her." He looked directly into Benard's eyes. "We also know that your family does not approve, but I insist that you lead the song next week."

Benard hesitated. "I will talk to my parents."

The two adults stiffened. "So will we."

"Distinguished Member of Parliament, we are so glad you have come," an enamored woman dressed in a freshly pressed skirt and blouse said.

Dozens of starry-eyed fans blocked the path toward the red velvet chair at the end of the aisle. All of them appeared smitten with the idea of being noticed by one with power, position, and money. Benard shook his head as the politician pasted on a smile and caught the attention of her guard, giving a nearly untraceable nod.

"Back, woman! Let your honored guest through," the guard shouted.

The crowd parted reluctantly, and the dignitary proceeded to take her seat. Frowning, she surveyed the crowd while fingering the ornate trim on the cuff of her sleeve. As Benard silently reviewed the lyrics, he noticed the guest smothering a yawn. Great.

Benard breathed deeply and forced his eyes to the front. He froze as he saw his music teacher looking for him, and with heart pounding, he hurried through the side door, into position. He beckoned from behind the curtain. "Teacher, I am ready now."

Moving backstage, the teacher smiled and waved his arm through the air. Background music instantly swirled around the uniformed students as they filed in and filled the risers. Beaming, Benard stood in front of them dressed in a borrowed but neatly pressed blue-and-white uniform. Teacher appeared soon after and placed a hand on Benard's shoulder.

"This is our prize pupil, Benard Ondiek. Benard has written a song for our honored guest."

All eyes swung from the stage to the red velvet throne, but the dignitary focused straight ahead. The politician lifted her hand and gave a slight nod. Applause filled the large canvas tent, and the teacher stepped down from the stage.

Turning to face the choir, Benard raised his hand and signaled the beginning of the song. His voice rang out loud and clear. After the song ended, he whipped back around in time to see the member of Parliament lean forward in her chair, seemingly astounded by what she heard. When the group finished performing, Benard turned in the politician's direction and bowed deeply. The Member of Parliament rose and motioned for Benard.

Benard made his way down the aisle, heart pounding. What would the woman say to him? Did she like it? Did she hate it? Moving directly in front of the dignitary, Benard glanced up. Could that possibly be a smile?

"Well done, Benard. You are a bright boy." The Member of Parliament's voice dripped with confidence. "Not only was the singing impressive, but the lyrics also proved remarkable. Your obvious intelligence and humble respect seeped into the song's content and created a masterpiece."

"Thank you, ma'am." Benard tried to keep from smiling but without success.

The politician studied the lad. "I will do something to help you continue your education, Benard."

"Oh, thank you!"

She smiled. "Thank you, Benard."

Having completed his secondary school education with a partial scholarship from the gracious dignitary, Benard walked the three hours down the dung-packed road for the last time.

"Mama, I'm done!" He burst into her bedroom and ran to her side. He smiled at the wan, unkempt woman he found. Wrinkled skin hung on her bony face. Perspiration drenched her curly hair, and the odor of ill health hung in the room.

"My son." Mama attempted to return his smile.

"Oh, Mama." Compassion swept over Benard as he reached for her paper-thin hand. Her eyelids drifted shut, and Benard made sure to cover her well. He wiped her brow with a cool rag from the basin.

"Mama," he whispered, "I am done with school, Mama. You will see. I will get a good job and take you to the doctor." He rose and stared down at her.

"You will see."

Chapter Four

Heart of Rock

Benard glared across the room. His roommate, Levi, sang and played his guitar as if the chords would disappear if he stopped. Benard wanted to scream but knew that trying to stop the outpouring of worship coming from the skinny young musician would prove futile.

For months, Benard had endured Levi's persistent playing, singing, and Bible reading. Even though Levi had a nice voice, his endless barrage irritated Benard. But Benard would rather move out than say anything.

Benard sighed. He really did not want to move out. Levi had shown him kindness from the day they had met in Levi's west Kenyan village where Benard was searching for work. Upon receiving a job offer in Levi's hometown, Benard had quickly accepted Levi's invitation to live with him, and now, over six hundred miles away from his home in Wachara, Benard realized that Levi had become his closest friend.

Levi stopped playing, his face filled with incredible joy. He glanced at Benard and quietly put the instrument away.

Benard smiled. Finally, some peace and quiet. He continued with his reading until Levi gently approached him.

"Excuse me, Benard," Levi said softly yet with confidence. "I don't want to bother you, but will you come to the big youth rally with me tonight? It's going to be so much fun! Please? I don't want to be a bother, but . . ."

"It is too late for that, my friend," Benard replied half-joking.

"Look, Benard, I really want you to come. All of the guys will be there. Pastor Wilson is speaking tonight, and I think you'd like him."

"Levi, I know you like the rallies, but I really don't want to go. You keep asking me, and I haven't said yes once in these four months I've lived with you."

"I know," Levi admitted, looking troubled. He rubbed his head and then bent to adjust his sandal.

Benard hesitated. He was hurting Levi's feelings. Maybe one time wouldn't matter . . . Maybe if he went tonight, Levi would stop his pestering.

"Okay, I'll go if you never ask me to go again."

Levi stood up. "Do you mean it, Benard? You'll come tonight?"

"Yes. Yes, I will go with you, Levi."

Levi clasped his hands together and then ran to fetch some hot milk. "Great! We will leave at sundown."

"I'll be ready," Benard promised. Finally, he would have peace.

The church was packed. Hundreds of young people poured inside, and many overflowed into a fenced grassy area. Levi and Benard walked up to the group, making their way over to the fence. So far, Levi had been all smiles, but now he seemed concerned.

"Benard, I have to go up front and play my guitar. Will you be okay?"

"Of course. I will sit in the back."

Relief covered Levi's face. He nodded and then jogged inside, his black instrument case bumping into the calves of unsuspecting bystanders.

Benard considered leaving but thought better of it. He had told Levi he would come, and so he would keep his vow. He would not disappoint Levi. Benard panned the scene, grunting. Everything here would annoy him, but he would stay.

As the evening wore on and the band began to play, the temptation to leave pursued Benard like a lion chasing an antelope. He did not want to be there. Why had he let Levi talk him into this, anyway? Shifting on the rough wooden seat, he watched with a stony countenance as Levi played and passionate voices joined him in song. When would this thing finish?

The room grew still. One by one, young people walked to the platform and shared what God had done in their lives.

"Jesus is my Savior."

"I am saved."

"I love Jesus. I thank Him for saving me."

Benard squirmed. His childhood teachers had taught him many things about this Jesus, but this was the first time Benard listened in order to understand. Most of him wanted to go home, but now, a tiny part of him needed an answer. *How can someone be saved?*

The pastor got up and read Isaiah 1:18:

> *"Come now, let us reason together,"*
>   *says the LORD.*
> *"Though your sins are like scarlet,*
>   *they will be as white as snow;*
> *though they are red like crimson,*
>   *they shall be like wool."*

Benard marveled. How could he listen to and feel God? How could he reason with the Lord? Filled with wonder, Benard prayed his first heart-felt prayer.

O God, please reason with me!

And He did.

"I want to pray for you if you want to accept Christ."

The pastor's voice startled Benard. Many people came forward crying. They knelt down and prayed. Benard searched the room in awe. He began thinking about his life as the pastor continued speaking.

"You are a good man, but you are a sinner. You think about how you can help other people without first allowing Christ to help you. Do you know you are lost?"

The question kept repeating itself inside Benard's head. *Do you know you are lost? Do you know you are lost?* His heart pounded, and his eyes welled with tears. *I am a sinner.*

Suddenly, he felt a sweeping pull in his chest and knew it was the power of God. He stood and walked toward the front, not knowing how to pray but trying anyway.

The pastor spotted him and passed over several others to kneel by Benard's side. "God, thank You for this man, and I pray You bless him."

As the band began a different tune, Benard felt a hand on his shoulder. He turned to see Levi kneeling beside him, tears streaming down his cheeks.

"I'm so glad you came tonight, brother," Levi said.

After they hugged, Benard looked at his friend and smiled wide. "Today, I know what salvation is all about."

Chapter Five

Journey of Faith

A h, welcome, Benard! We are so happy to have you," said Pastor
Wilson Mattai. He swept his hand in front of his thin frame.
"Do come in."

Benard smiled his thanks, knowing it would never be enough. He
contemplated how he owed this man his life as he entered his mentor's humble dwelling.

"Good evening, Pastor Wilson."

"Come and sit, Benard."

He took his place at the table across from Pastor Wilson and
smiled again.

"You seem eager to begin, my friend." Pastor Wilson chuckled.
Clasping his hands in front of him, he beckoned Benard to imitate his
actions.

"Father God," he prayed, "we praise and thank You for saving
Benard and bringing him here day after day to study Your Word.
Open his heart and fill him with Your Holy Spirit that You may teach
him great things and produce bountiful fruit in this new Christian.
Bless our time together we pray, in Jesus' name. Amen."

"Amen," Benard echoed. He grinned, eager to begin his studies.
They planned to examine the book of John and continue to memorize various passages of Scripture.

Benard loved this! He could not wait to read about Nicodemus and how Jesus taught him in the middle of the night.

Instead of opening the Bible as Benard expected, Pastor Wilson folded his hands and looked at Benard with tired eyes. His shoulders drooped, and dark circles hung under his eyes.

"Benard, do you know why I take so much time to teach you all of these things?"

Benard shook his head. "No, you are a busy man."

Pastor Wilson observed his young pupil's expression.

"With only one pastor for every nine churches in Kenya, the pastors quickly burn out ministering to so many. Pastoring is a great responsibility, one for which few have the Bible knowledge and compassionate heart that the call requires.

"Therefore, the people suffer without a shepherd." His voice trembled and tears spilled down his cheeks. "Women lose their husbands, children lose their parents, sickness and poverty plague their homes . . . so much suffering, without a pastor to pray with them and encourage their tired spirits, to tell them God loves them and cares about their pain, to tell them the Good News of Jesus Christ."

Benard felt his pain. For weeks, Pastor Wilson had taken him and a meager food supply to a nearby village to minister to the people there. Small huts with thatched roofs lined the perimeter of a clearing located about forty minutes away by car. The village reeked of poor hygiene, decaying sewage, and wood smoke. While dirty children played in the grass, their emaciated parents either lay weak from fever on brown mats or worked from sunup to sundown caring for the sick.

Bending down on one knee, Pastor Wilson prayed with each sick person in the village while Benard watched and handed out the small loaves of ugali. The people clung to the pastor, some reaching out their hands to touch him. Benard's discomfort eased as he witnessed their pain melt away with the prayers and gentleness of the pastor. He found himself wishing he could give the same help and hope to the hurting around him.

Pastor Wilson wiped his tears, and his eyes began to shine with hope.

"Benard, I see discipleship as the key to the future of the church.

Without more trained pastors, the church as we know it will die. That is why I train you, Benard. God has given you many gifts for learning and ministering, and I believe He has an amazing plan for your life in the ministry."

Benard tried to take it all in.

"Me? But how? I know so little... how can God use me in these ways to help the people?" He felt perplexed yet hopeful. Pastor Wilson had never lied to him. Maybe with more training...

Pastor Wilson rose and walked around the tiny table. He placed a worn hand on Benard's strong shoulder.

"You are my son in the faith, Benard. I will teach you all that I can. After that, I want you to go to Kapsabet Bible College and learn all you can about the Bible so that you can teach the people and train more pastors."

Over the next four years, Benard shadowed Pastor Wilson as he went from village to village visiting widows and orphans, praying with the sick, and helping those in need. Sometimes they brought loaves of ugali or chipati, but today, food was scarce.

As Benard and Pastor Wilson arrived in the village of the Kalanjin tribe, they found themselves praying fervently for protection because an eerie darkness hung in the air all around them. The people eyed them suspiciously, and some even insulted them verbally. A tall, brazen warrior strode up to them and demanded to know the business of the two men.

Pastor Wilson had warned Benard about this hostile tribe the night before.

> Over four hundred years ago, the leaders from the Luo tribe and the Kalanjin tribe met around a campfire in the village of the Luo. The two tribes had enjoyed a peaceful relationship, but that terrible night, everything changed.
>
> The men became engrossed in a heated discussion, so much so that a young girl slipped a small

leather pouch from the belt of the Kalanjin's chieftain. The child ran off and uncovered her booty—the sacred bead which the Kalanjin clan believed to hold special powers. She marveled at her treasure, forgetting the looming danger in the midst of her great adventure.

Within minutes, the chieftain discovered his loss and began calling curses down upon the perpetrator. The girl panicked when she heard loud footsteps approaching her hut and shoved the pouch under a sleeping mat, realizing too late that her sweaty palm still clutched the sacred bead.

As the door burst open, the child swallowed the bead. Warriors from both tribes rushed in, seized the girl, and tore apart the room. Mayhem broke loose, and the girl's parents grabbed her by her clothing, yanking her free. Luo warriors forced the Kalanjin back as the two sides screamed curses down upon each other.

A furious Kalanjin tribesman yelled at the Luo chieftain, waving the recovered leather pouch through the air. His eyes blazed, and he commanded that his chieftain's bead be returned immediately. The Luo chieftain assured him that their tribe would return the bead once the child eliminated it. Although the entire episode greatly desecrated the sacred bead and its powers, the Kalanjin appeared willing to accept its return.

Days went by, and the Luo girl did not pass the bead as expected. Terror grew each day as they waited for the return of the hostile Kalanjin chieftain. The Luo people claimed they wanted no trouble and apologized profusely for the wrong done, offering many cows, trinkets, gifts—even beads.

But not the one he wanted.

He wanted the girl dead and the sacred bead extracted.

The Luo people called a meeting, killed the child,

and extracted the bead. The two tribes have fought ever since.

Four hundred years later, the two warring tribes continue to pass on their hatred of each other to their children all because of the sacred bead. The feud has erected walls in communication, progress, and peace in the surrounding communities.

Pastor Wilson gazed at Benard. "I believe peace between these two tribes is possible through Jesus Christ." He paused.

"They need a church, Benard, and I believe the Lord will have you plant one among the Kalanjin someday. My load is too great, but you, my young friend, you have the energy to do the work church planting requires. I will pray for you, and when you finish at Kapsabet Bible College, maybe you will go to these people with a message of peace. Tomorrow, we will visit them."

Pastor Wilson closed his eyes as if in prayer.

"Maybe they will allow us to preach in the village."

Pamela

Chapter Six

Pamela

FOUR YEARS LATER ~ 1989

*T*hank You, Father, for the opportunity to finish Bible college and plant a church! Benard smiled as he spoke with the Lord. *I never dreamed it would require so much hard work, but You have led me every step of the way. Please give me strength to persevere in obedience to You, my Lord. I pray all of this in the name of the Lord Jesus Christ. Amen.*

Brushing dirt from the knees of his trousers, Benard rose. There was no better way to start the day than ignited by the power of prayer. *Every day, Lord,* he had vowed. *I will start every day with You.*

Footsteps pattered up to his door.

"Benard, are you done praying?" asked Pastor Wilson.

"Come in, Pastor Wilson," Benard called, eyeing with curiosity the smiling older gentleman who seemed to sprint across the room. Benard closed the door, and the two sat cross-legged on woven floor mats.

"How is your mother doing, Benard?"

Concern spread across Benard's face. "She is not well, Pastor Wilson. Her sickness has begun to bend her legs." Tears formed in Benard's eyes. "She will not be able to walk soon according to the doctor in Kisumu."

"I'm sorry, Benard." Pastor Wilson bit his lip and swallowed hard. "I will continue to pray for her."

Benard sensed his mentor had come with joyful news, so Benard gave a small smile. "Mama has found Christ, Pastor Wilson. She will be okay." Benard studied his visitor and waited.

Pastor Wilson could contain himself no longer. "Benard!" The pastor inhaled then exhaled, closing his eyes briefly. He tried again. "Benard, you have done well here among the tribal people. One church planted—praise the Lord!" Pastor Wilson's radiant face matched Benard's.

"Praise God, indeed. I could not have done any of it without Him. Church planting holds tremendous challenges."

Pastor Wilson nodded his agreement. "That is why I am here, Benard. My pastoral group has been asked to select one pastor to speak at the regional youth rally in a couple of weeks, and we have unanimously nominated you."

Benard busied himself with a kettle of hot milk and two mugs until he found his tongue.

"Ah, thank you, Pastor Wilson. I consider it an honor to speak and pray that the Lord gives me a message that will reach the hearts of the young people for Jesus Christ."

Pastor Wilson slapped his back with glee. "You will do fine, Benard," he said with assurance. "God will go before you and prepare their hearts. I realize you have not spoken to this large of a group before, but the experience will prove helpful to you."

Holding out a hand, Pastor Wilson accepted the steamy beverage and took a large gulp. "Besides, you are a young man, a spring chicken compared to us old roosters. The kids will listen to you like a friend, not a father."

Deep in thought, Benard stared into the fire.

Pastor Wilson chuckled. "You're not going to hear another word I say because your mind is already spinning with topics."

Suddenly shy, Benard smiled. "I'm sorry, Pastor Wilson."

The seasoned pastor waved a hand. "Do not worry, Benard. Your enthusiasm blesses me. God will use it for good in the lives of the youth. Remember how He used a youth rally in your life?"

Pastor Wilson drained his cup and stood. "I will leave so that the Holy Spirit can speak to your soul. May the Lord bless you, my son," he said as he shook Benard's hand.

Benard's eyes sparkled. "May the Lord bless you, Pastor Wilson."

Amazed, Benard surveyed the teens pouring into the church. How many young people lived in this city? They must all be here tonight. Thankful that he had arrived early, he looked around for the woman who had helped him set up earlier that day.

She was not only beautiful, but she also had keen eyes and a wise manner. Benard had been watching. Throughout the day, he had noticed that when the pastor in charge of the event had continually sought her out to ask questions about the stage set up, refreshments, and schedule, the intriguing volunteer always had an answer and showed a deep respect for her pastor. Upon Benard's arrival, the pastor immediately introduced her.

"Benard, you must know Pamela. She will help you, as she does me, with anything you need. You may have to search for her because she's always bustling about, but we couldn't organize or run such an event without her."

Benard sensed Pamela's blush under the high praise and attempted to ease her discomfort with a few questions about setting up. She seemed grateful and snapped into work mode. Before she left to assist another volunteer, she smiled at Benard.

"Thank you for speaking tonight."

The innocent way in which she looked at him caused heat to surge through his body. She walked away, but his eyes followed her. What a remarkable lady. Even the pastor thought so. Somehow, Benard gathered himself and made his way to the platform, stealing another peek at her talking to a cluster of volunteers across the sanctuary. Her words appeared to calm and reassure them.

He must inquire about her.

Benard floated off the stage. *O God of Heaven, I praise You for the souls You won tonight! Thank You for such a chance to be a small part of what You're doing in the hearts of people!*

Many young people had come forward at Benard's invitation and accepted Jesus Christ as their Savior. The experience reminded him of his own conversion only ten years earlier.

There she is! Pamela stood five feet away praying with an older woman. His heart fluttered, the intensity of it forcing him to take a deep breath. Was there anything this woman could not do? He squirmed as they stopped praying and observed him watching them.

Playing the part of the ever-sensitive hostess, Pamela excused herself and hastened to his side. "Did you need something, Pastor Benard?"

His parched throat managed to squeak out a reply. "Thank you, Sister Pamela. Thank you for all of your help tonight."

She glowed. "Many came to the Lord. Thank you for being a willing vessel."

He smiled at her, trying to gather the courage to do what he believed he must. *Please help me with the words, Lord.*

"Pamela," he began, "can I write to you? I would like to keep in touch."

The air crackled with emotion as Benard waited for her response. She seemed surprised but masked her feelings. Finally, she spoke.

"Yes, you may write to me, Benard," she said, venturing to use his first name. She pulled a pen from behind her ear and jotted her address on a slip of paper she drew from her Bible.

I don't believe this is happening, Father! She's giving it to me! His heart leapt with joy. *She wants me to write to her!* He tried to smother his eager ear-to-ear grin, but when she looked at him and said goodbye, he beamed.

"Good night, Pamela. You will hear from me soon."

Grumpiness got the best of him. For months, Benard had written letters to Pamela but had not received one note, letter, or postcard. Nothing. When he had completed the church-planting process, he returned to town to prepare for his next assignment. Reaching into his mailbox, he could not suppress his hope that today would be different. He shuffled through the bills and memos.

Nothing.

He sighed. *What shall I do, Lord?* He walked into his bedroom at Pastor Wilson's house, closed the door, and hunkered down on the floor. His heart had grown heavier each day as he prayed for Pamela and how to handle the awkward situation. She did not seem like the type of girl who would play with a man's heart. No, definitely not. *Maybe something has happened...*

Father, only You know what's going on with Pamela. Please show me what You want me to do about this, for I cannot stop thinking about her.

Go find her.

Benard trembled.

The sun cast a magnificent light over dozens of colorful dresses, skirts, and shawls that lined the corner booth in the marketplace. Orange and blue, khaki and amethyst, gold and magenta. Bolt after bolt of fabric and lace lay on the display table, tantalizing passersby to order something custom-made.

Pamela sat behind the table hemming a cotton green-and-white skirt, thinking about another letter she had received from Benard last week. It was a shame he lived so far away. Her pastor had shared some of Benard's church-planting background with her, acquainting her with the faraway tribes he had touched.

What her pastor meant for encouragement actually disheartened the young woman. Benard couldn't be serious about her. He was in no position to take a wife, for surely a wife would distract him from his calling. Even though Pamela had enjoyed serving with him the evening of their meeting, she had accepted the impossibility of a continued relationship.

Her hand guided the needle through the last stitch and knotted her thread. Snip. Cutting the end, she sighed and forced her thoughts away from Benard and onto the red-and-blue striped gown for a Member of Parliament's wife. Many dresses awaited her attention, and Papa would soon return, expecting them finished. Maybe then he would let her go buy some bananas for lunch . . .

"Hello, Pamela."

She froze at the deep baritone voice. *Benard!* Her pulse quickened as she saw him standing in front of the booth. His shirt was neatly pressed, and his countenance appeared confident.

"Hello, Benard." She laid her needlework aside and stood. "How did you find me?"

He fingered the sleeve of a rust-colored gown. "It was not easy. I almost turned back because I thought I had checked all of the booths in the market."

Pamela did not know what to say. Her mind had grown fuzzy at the sight of him, and now she could barely breathe at his disclosure. Had he come down to find her?

"Why are you here?"

He looked into her eyes. "I have to know why you have not returned my letters. Is everything okay with you and your family?"

"Um, yes, my family and I are well."

His face fell.

She hurried on, surprised by the impact of her words. "Benard, I did not write you back because I didn't understand how you could be thinking seriously about me. You live so far away—"

"Pamela," he said, holding up a palm, "I asked if I could write to you. I would not play a game with your heart and start something I had no intention of finishing right."

Hope filled her heart, and she confessed everything.

"Pastor told me that you live with remote tribes planting churches . . . which is wonderful, but I didn't see how we could build a relationship with such a situation. You see, I . . . I did not want to get in the way of what God wanted to do with your life."

His full smile warmed her down to the tips of her toes.

"Pamela, I wish to speak to your parents. Today. I want to ask permission to marry you. I only have two cows to offer for your dowry—"

"Today?" Her hand flew to her chest. Mama would have a fit! "But they will not be prepared—"

"It will be okay, Pamela," he said in a calm voice. "I will talk to your father about everything and respect what he has to say to me. The matter is in the Lord's hands."

Pamela rubbed her expanding stomach with delight. The baby within her womb gave a hearty kick and took her breath away. She gathered the last three shirts from the line and headed back inside. Exactly one year ago on May 25, 1991, Pastor Benard Ondiek had made her his bride at his parents' home in Wachara. The couple now lived at the site of Benard's second church plant but had spent the last few days making preparations to move to the village of the Kalanjin tribe.

Pastor Wilson had long ago planted a seed that furrowed a tender spot in Benard's heart for the Kalanjin people. Benard knew the risks involved, especially bringing a wife and soon-to-be-born child into an actively warring tribe. He also knew that God had clearly led them there.

Rustling through the baskets and bags on the table, Pamela extracted pieces of chapati to eat with the goat meat the villagers had given them as a farewell gift. She wanted to be ready with dinner when Benard arrived. Morning would come quickly, and she predicted he would want to rise early.

Her excitement grew by the second. *I can't wait to see what You're going to do in that place, Lord.*

Chapter Seven

Night of Terror

LATER THAT YEAR ~ 1992

*T*asty smells filled Benard's nostrils. He followed the scent of ugali and beef stew into the tiny thatched-roof hut located on the outskirts of the Kalanjin village. Bending down, he entered the dark, earthy-smelling room and gazed at his lovely Pamela while she tended their young son, Abraham. She glanced up and smiled, tucking a stray lock behind her ear.

"Welcome home, Benard. Would you like something to eat?"

He nodded.

She turned and stirred a big black cauldron hanging over the open fire.

Benard's heart filled with love as he watched her. She worked so hard, taking care of the baby and cooking.

The baby gurgled and reached for his father. Benard lifted him from Pamela's arms and furrowed his brow as he thought over the day. Four years at Kapsabet Bible College and planting three churches had not prepared him for the heated exchange he'd had with the tribal leadership at dawn.

Dressed for war, many scowling village men made an appearance, all of them carrying knives or handguns. Some demanded they kill Benard immediately. Fear had washed over him.

Lord God, give me words! How should I speak to these people? Protect me, I pray.

Not once had he felt at home here among the Kalanjin, a clan that had treated him and Pamela harshly from day one. Facing the hostile audience, Benard reiterated that he sought peace and had no intention of causing trouble.

Over a great fire, the men explained their concerns about Benard and Pamela starting a church among the Kalanjin people. Even though he and Pamela had lived in their hut for a few months, they had not earned enough trust to start a church. The people clung to ancient superstitions and traditions, refusing to accept the Ondieks and their invisible God.

Benard sighed, his spirit downtrodden. He would tell Pamela after dinner. They would eat in peace and then ask the Lord what He would have them do. Benard believed a church plant would thrive here once the people gave the Gospel a fair hearing. Ever since Pastor Wilson had shared the bead story with Benard, he had wanted to plant a church here.

But now, the future appeared uncertain.

"Come, Benard," Mama Pamela said, her voice gentle. "Eat your dinner."

Benard stood with her alongside the crude table, easing the baby back into her arms.

"Father God, we worship You. You are a great God, and we praise You for Your blessings and the love You have shown us through Your Son, Jesus Christ. Thank You for this food. Please nourish our bodies with it, and help us to trust You this very day. In the name of Jesus. Amen."

"Amen."

They sat and began to eat in comfortable silence, watching little Abraham giggle with delight between mouthfuls.

Pamela glanced at Benard. "How did the council meeting go this morning?"

Does the woman miss nothing?

"It did not go well. The people are angry with us for coming here and trying to change their ways. I don't know what they will do."

Benard scooped up a bite of stew but then leapt to his feet as the door to their tiny hut flew open. A huge warrior with a painted face thrust his spear toward Benard's face as three more warriors entered. *O God, please help me! What do they want?* He recognized the men as Kalanjin leaders, dressed for war.

War with me?

The chieftain arrived. Benard searched their faces and saw their fear. *O Lord, I pray I am not the cause of such fear!*

Raising his aged walking stick, the elderly chieftain shook it at Benard. "You and your family must leave, or we will kill you. Take everything with you!"

Benard held out his hands. "We must talk—"

The stubborn chief waved his arm in disgust. "No more talk. You go." He paced the beaten path outside Benard's door as he spoke. "Two tribes want to make war with us because they think we are listening to you and turning our backs on the traditions of our fathers. You have brought trouble upon us." He drew close to Benard's face and spat on him.

"We never asked you to come here. You are not welcome in our village anymore. We will not be responsible for the blood they believe must be shed to purify us from our wandering ways."

Benard's heart pounded, and his mouth felt thick and dry. "Please, you must understand."

A warrior grabbed his arm. "There is no time, Benard. They are coming now to kill you."

Out of the corner of his eye, he saw Pamela bustling about gathering essentials and bundling baby Abraham. She slung him onto her back and tied the knot of her blue shawl around her slender neck. Benard drew strength from his sensible wife's actions and bolted to her. He grasped her upper arm firmly and cupped the bundle containing their only son.

"Pamela, you must go now. These men will help me transport our things, but you and the baby must leave now."

To her credit, Pamela nodded and obeyed.

"I will show her the way," said a small voice.

Benard turned to find a young girl standing at his elbow. Pamela had befriended the youngest orphan in the tribe by asking her to help care for Abraham on occasion, and now the girl seemed eager to help her friends.

Pamela followed the girl to the door and took one last, long look at Benard standing in the doorway before slipping away into the night.

Benard wept inside. *Lord, watch over my Pamela. My young Abraham . . . he is small and hungry. Please keep him quiet and use this girl to lead them to safety.* Goose bumps covered his arms and legs, causing shivers to erupt down his spine. He eyed the tree line, uncertain who might already be lurking in its shadows. *Protect me, Lord. Send a mighty band of angels to surround this place.*

Back inside, the tribesmen seemed to have come to an agreement about how to manage Benard's possessions. The chief stepped forward.

"We will carry—"

A spear struck the door three inches to the left of Benard's head. He saw the point through the rickety wood slat as he fell to his knees and rolled under the small table laden with cold stew. All of the men including the chief rushed out of the hut except one, Benard's guard.

While war cries and deafening screams of women and children filled the village, the remaining warrior jammed the door shut with a stool. Heavy footsteps pounded outside but none approached Benard's door. *O God, O God, help us! Help the people, please,* Benard prayed.

At that moment, he realized he should have fled with Pamela. *What am I doing, Lord? What good will our belongings do us if I perish tonight?* His stomach turned as he thought of Pamela running for her life through the wild with a baby slowing her down and a little girl as her guide.

O God, please help them!

Pamela gulped for air as she braced herself against a tree. *How much farther, Lord?* Abraham cried softly, and she whipped the bundle on her back around to her stomach. Without a word, she held him close to buffer the sound. *Please don't cry, my love, not now.* She retied the know around her weary neck, deciding to front-carry him until they left this dangerous territory.

The young girl guide had waved at Pamela to stop some minutes before and edged up the path alone. *An eternity has gone by, Lord. Where is she?*

Pamela brushed her palm over her forehead. All of her skin longed for a thorough scratching, but she didn't dare indulge. Any movement might give her position away to the enemies lurking in the darkness.

Deep rumbling startled her until she identified it as her own hunger pangs. She ignored them and tried not to think about her cotton mouth or the cuts on her bare feet. *Father, sustain me. Please, God, protect my Abraham.* She struggled not to weep. *And my Benard, Lord. Be with Benard.*

The girl had been gone too long. Crouching low, Pamela crept into the darkness looming before her. *Lord God, keep Abraham quiet. Please help us, Lord. Help us!* Her prayers rose to heaven with each step. She felt unseen eyes watching and waiting, and her knees quivered at the thought of capture. The tribal people were savages. They would surely kill a frightened mother and baby.

Out of the deep brush, someone grabbed her arm and yanked her to the ground. Pamela struggled to get away as a hand clasped over her mouth. In the moonlight, she saw the somber face of her trail guide, the little girl from the village. Relief washed over Pamela as the girl gestured for silence. Pamela nodded and drew the baby closer to her body, attempting to shield him from whatever lurked on the path ahead.

As they waited, Pamela's senses tuned into signals hidden within the beautiful scenery around them. A hoot. Two small whistles. Shaking branches and crackling wood. *O God! They're everywhere!* Panic rose in her throat as the girl beside her studied everything, giving no indication she planned to move anytime soon.

Be still, Pamela, for I am with you.

The assurance calmed Pamela's heart. *Lord, do not leave us! Protect us! Help us get away.*

Baby Abraham stirred. He would be hungry soon, and nursing him here would surely reveal their hiding place. To her credit, the guide noticed Abraham's unrest and, after breathing deeply, appeared to make a decision. She motioned to Pamela to return to the trail but also to keep low. She nodded and obeyed.

As she stepped out, three warriors crept out of the brush about eighteen meters up the path. Pamela froze. *O God!* The little girl stayed put, her eyes wide with fear. Pamela began to tremble and prayed with all her might.

A banging, crashing noise to the right of the men drew their attention, and they disappeared in the thick brush on the opposite side of the trail without having so much as glanced her way. Filled with hope, Pamela reached for the girl's hand. Without a sound, they sped down the path, never looking back.

Smoke from burning grass filled Benard's nostrils as he packed up their few belongings. The guard at the door told Benard that the invaders had set fire to most of the huts in the village and would soon arrive.

"Here they come," the guard warned, backing away from the small opening he had cut in the wall of the hut. Benard rushed to the peephole and gasped. *O God! There are so many. What should I do?*

The guard looked at him with intense loathing, and Benard wondered if he would live to see the hut burn down around him. Tears formed but would not run. *O God, help me! Help me!*

Be still, Benard.

Instantly, he felt peace wash over his spirit. He turned to the young man who risked his life by staying with him. "It will be all right."

The man glared and returned to the peephole. Within minutes, he spoke in excited tones. "They're leaving! They have spared your house." He grabbed Benard's arm and shook hard, knife in hand. "Go now! Leave, or I will kill you!"

He shoved Benard toward the door and pushed him outside, calling down curses upon him until he ran out of sight, back into the deserted, blazing section of the village.

Lord, what now? Benard gasped for breath as staggered over uneven ground strewn with clothing, severed mattresses, and spilled food supplies. While war cries echoed through the night, Benard clung to the few possessions Pamela had gathered for him and searched for an escape, a way out of this wretched mess. A thick haze hovered over the remnants of the village, bringing tears to his burning eyes. Benard stood in the middle of ransacked, burning ruins and raised his eyes toward the heavens. From the depths of his soul, he cried, "O God! Help me! Please help me!"

The steady hum of a two-liter engine broke into the terrifying night. Benard saw a man driving straight toward him, motioning frantically out the half-open window. The visitor whipped open the passenger door and screamed at Benard.

"Get in the car! Hurry! Get in the car!" His eyes darted over Benard's shoulder.

Benard followed the driver's glance and took in the gathering band of warriors in the distance now aware of the waiting vehicle.

"NOW!"

Benard flew to the white jalopy, gripped the doorframe, and hurled his body into the front seat. The mysterious driver slammed the accelerator as an arrow ricocheted off the passenger door, now flapping madly back and forth. Benard flung his books, pictures, and clothing onto the floor and clenched the dashboard with both hands. Groaning and whirring, the car did a one-eighty and raced toward the path leading to the dung road out of the village.

"Hang on!" The driver clenched the wheel with both hands and sat tense and upright in his worn seat.

Tribesmen poured out of the brush and pursued them, hollering threats and chanting incantations to their gods. Arrows and spears soared through the air but none touched the fleeing pair.

Benard continued to clutch the dashboard with his left hand, as he reached back with his right to fasten the seatbelt. The jerky driving maneuvers threw him off balance twice and forced him to hold on to the dashboard with both hands. Click. The seatbelt somehow locked into place. Benard reached for the car door and tugged it shut. *Thank You, God!* Wiping his brow, he glanced in the mirror and noticed the warriors' retreat.

"They're going back, friend."

The driver, a slender wisp of a man appearing to be in his forties, surveyed the rearview mirror. He closed his eyes for a split second. "Praise God!"

Silence surrounded the duo as they eased onto the soft dung road. Adrenaline surged through Benard's veins, making him want to run down the road instead of ride into town and to Pamela.

Pamela. O God, Pamela! Where is she? His thoughts raged, making him feel like a caged beast. *I must find her.* Helplessness engulfed him, and he turned to his companion.

"We must find my wife."

For the first time, the driver smiled. "You will find her, my friend."

Benard wished he shared the man's confidence.

The Lord is my light and my salvation; whom shall I fear? The Lord is the stronghold of my life; of whom shall I be afraid?

Pamela silently recited verse after verse, attempting to calm the unrest within her spirit. The girl clung to her side, no longer a confident guide but a scared child.

I must feed the baby. Pamela knew Abraham would cry soon for her milk. *Hush, little one. Not much longer.* She hoped. Her eyes searched out a hiding place nestled deep in a patch of tall grass. Using a light squeeze, Pamela signaled the girl to follow her inside. Both collapsed and clung to the other without a word. Abraham stirred. Pamela quickly unbundled him and positioned him for nursing. Back in their little hut, she had always considered his suckle silent, but now, it sounded louder than a hundred thirsty dogs lapping water.

She placed her shawl over his face, muffling the sound. She sighed, thankful for the small reprieve.

The little girl looked dreadful in the moonlight. Her clothes were torn, her skin gashed from sharp tree branches, and her arms and legs covered with welts from insect bites. Pamela patted her arm, and the girl ventured a smile. She relaxed, but suddenly her eyes widened in fear as she pointed to a pair of reddish eyes.

Pamela froze. Rats. A dozen red eyes dotted the outskirts of their refuge. *O God!* In one fluid motion, she reached into her blouse, broke Abraham's seal, and pulled the shawl around him. The girl had already rushed out of the bushes and onto the trail. Pamela followed, and they hurried as fast as they could. Glancing over her shoulder, Pamela's heart began to pound as the rats scurried after them in hot pursuit.

"Run!" Pamela broke the silent code and pushed the girl ahead of her as she felt teeth sink into her ankles and calves. *O God! O God! Please, help us!* Warm blood oozed over her chilled skin, turning her stomach. Frantically, she kicked her feet, attempting to dislodge the invaders. Her haphazard technique worked somewhat, and she tore ahead into what seemed to be a clearing.

The road! Pamela's heart beat with hope. *Maybe someone will stop to help us! Where is the girl? Maybe there . . . O Lord, no!*

The little girl huddled in a ball at the end of the path with four warriors from the Mattai tribe towering over her and glaring at Pamela's approach.

Two men came out of the bushes behind her and thrust her forward.

"We must kill you and your children," the leader said.

Pamela's knees shook as she gazed into his eyes. "Why?"

"You have polluted the Kalanjin with your lies, and we must purge all who taunt the traditions of our fathers." Cheers rose from his companions as they waved their spears and knives through the air, one swerving close to Pamela's head.

Two beams of light pierced the darkness. In the distance, a soft hum drew the tribesmen's attention away from their captives. Pamela reached for the girl's hand and clasped it tight. *Lord, please, please!*

A sputtering two-door white jalopy pulled up, and a thin young man hopped out. His pressed shirt, pleated slacks, and polished shoes exuded unspoken order.

"Mama, you must come with me," he said. His tone was calm, his demeanor peaceful. "Come with me." He opened his door and then picked up the wide-eyed little girl.

The warriors stood still, stunned. Pamela seized the opportunity and bolted to the car, sliding all the way over.

After placing the girl on the seat beside Pamela, the mysterious driver jumped in and drove away from the open-mouthed warriors who had begun shouting curses after them.

Pamela thanked the driver through her tears when she saw the town come into view. With dawn approaching, her body shook as chills consumed her. She pulled the dozing girl closer.

Their rescuer gazed at the tender scene. "You are safe now, my friends."

Benard tried not to panic. *Where was she?* He had looked everywhere. Churches, restaurants, stores, even the police station which offered little help to civilians no longer in danger. He didn't want to ask the question, but he found himself wondering. *Had she made it? And what of little Abraham and the girl?* Sleep had eluded him for the past two days as he searched for his family. Would he ever see them again?

What should I do, Lord?

With a heavy heart and sagging eyelids, Benard stumbled to a bench bordering the university. Exhaustion took over, and he slept until a young man shook his arm.

"Wake up, wake up. Are you Benard?" The lad spoke with great excitement.

Benard swung his legs to the ground. "I am Benard."

"Come with me."

The young man wasted no time weaving to and fro through the streams of pedestrians. A sleepy Benard struggled to keep up but pressed on, assuming his companion had information about his family. They slowed in front of a tin shack. The door opened, and the little guide ran into Benard's arms.

"Pastor Benard, you've come for us!"

He embraced her and carried her into the dim recesses of the home.

"Pamela?" He voiced the question before he saw her lying on a thin mat covered with her blue shawl. As she waved from the corner, he noticed the white bandages streaked with blood adorning her ankles and calves. He fell to his knees beside her and drew her into his arms along with the girl who refused to let go of him.

"Oh, Pamela," he whispered, stroking her hair and breathing in the scent of her. *Thank You, God! Thank You, God!* He pulled away and cupped her face in his hand, staring at the beautiful woman he thought he had lost on the trail.

Her tired eyes sparkled for only a moment. The great pain returned and claimed her, forcing her to lie back on the mattress as tears streamed down her cheeks. She sobbed as she recounted their horrible journey.

Benard heard a soft gurgle. Only then did he notice Abraham, nestled in a corner of her light blue shawl. Relief, joy, and pain rolled through the chambers of his spirit, and the sobs he had withheld for the eternity of their terror-filled night unleashed deep within.

He scooped up Abraham with his free arm, wiped Pamela's tears, and stroked the young girl's hair as they wept together. After a time, Benard bowed his head.

"O God, thank You for bringing us safely out of danger. It was Your power that kept the men from coming into the house in the village. It was You who sent the drivers to rescue us. It was You who brought our family back together. Thank You, Lord . . ."

His voice broke. He had no more words.

Chapter Eight

A New Beginning

Pools of sweat drenched Pamela's feverish body. Her husband stood nearby wringing out yet another cool cloth to place on her forehead.

Sweet Benard, how he found time to care for her, Abraham, and the little girl guide as well as the rest of the ministry she would never know. She longed to be up and about, caring for her household, but the poison from the rat bites had left her legs swollen and her walk impaired.

Due to fevers from the infection, Pamela's recovery period had dragged on month after month, causing a great strain on the young pastor. To his credit, he complained not once. "It is my honor to care for you, Pamela," he would say when she fretted about not feeling well enough to cook and clean. "Please let me enjoy serving you today."

Abraham stirred and cried out in his sleep. His father hurried to comfort him, holding the boy tight. "There, there little one."

Pamela marveled at Benard's stamina, fearing at times that he too would take ill. So far, the Lord had kept them in the palm of His hand, providing for all their needs.

Sleep captured both of its victims. Benard allowed himself a tired yet contented sigh as he put Abraham back into bed and took a seat near Pamela who was dozing.

What a day, Lord, what a day! Thank You that Pamela seemed to have more energy today than yesterday. He wiped her face with a cool rag, trying not to rouse her. Tears clouded his vision. *Thank You for helping us survive that horrible night and leading us back together. That was a terrible time for us, Lord.*

Stretching his arms over his head, Benard shook off his shoes. He must rest. His family would need him in the morning. Benard eased his frame onto the thin mat next to Pamela's and expected to drift right off, but sleep did not come. Worry threatened to take hold, so Benard chose to pray instead of succumb.

Please heal my wife, Lord God! She is so uncomfortable ... it is hard for me to see her this way. Should we go home to Wachara as planned?

The little girl guide had been returned safely to her village, but how would he get Pamela home unnoticed in her condition? And with a baby?

O Lord, I ask You to provide work for me and food for our table. Only one small hunk of ugali remains for their breakfast. Increase our faith, Father, for we trust in You ...

"Pastor Wilson, how are you? We are thrilled that you have come. Please," said Benard, motioning for his spiritual father to enter their temporary dwelling. *O God, could this be Your answer?*

Pastor Wilson seemed full of sunshine.

"Benard! You have no idea how difficult it was to locate you after the tribal clash with all the breaks in communication for miles around. I was so relieved to hear you are safe and will be moving back to Wachara. Thank You, Father!"

Pastor Wilson hugged Benard warmly, commenting in a fatherly way about the dark circles outlining his bloodshot eyes.

Benard said nothing, averting his eyes.

"You've done an excellent job hiding your family from your enemies."

A chill ran down Benard's spine. Even though the greatest danger had passed, it was too soon to feel completely safe.

Pastor Wilson turned and strode into the room where Pamela lay. He wept upon seeing the once robust young wife and mother lying helpless while the world carried on around her.

"Mama Pamela, I am sorry you have been so sick. My wife and I have prayed for you every day."

"Thank you, Pastor Wilson," she managed to mumble, smiling weakly. "May the Lord bless you."

Shuffling his feet and rubbing his forearm, Pastor Wilson glanced at Benard.

"Maybe I shouldn't have come, but I have to try. We need you."

Benard tilted his head. What was Pastor Wilson trying to say? He made no sense.

"Pamela, after you and Benard spend a few months recovering in Wachara, I want you and Benard to come to Ahero with me." The pastor gave the couple little time to absorb his statement.

"The fellowship of Ahero pastors believes that God is leading us to start a seminary. Kenya needs more pastors. Both of you know the demands of the ministry and how few pastors feel qualified and physically able to train more to follow in their footsteps.

"Benard, we want to put you in charge, give you a small salary, and ask you to teach the bulk of the courses. We will help, but the school will be yours to oversee and the curriculum yours to develop."

Pastor Wilson's kind eyes shifted to Pamela. "This way, Mama Pamela will be near more women who can help care for both her and Abraham."

Benard gulped and stared at Pamela.

Pastor Wilson choked back tears as he waved his hand through the air. "Let me take all of you out of this wretched place."

Benard and Pamela both wept. *Thank You, God!*

Benard recovered first. "We didn't know what to do . . ."

Pastor Wilson walked over to Benard and placed a firm hand on his shoulder. "Let's take you home, my son."

The Quest of a Kenyan Pastor ~ 67

"Your wife is much improved," Pastor Wilson's wife commented after the Sunday service. "Pregnancy seems to agree with her."

Benard joined her in watching his healthy, rounding Pamela speak with the other women in the sanctuary. He glowed. "Thank you, Mama. She has felt well for several weeks now. God used Ahero to heal her."

He nodded and moved down the pew towards the eleven students of the 1994 Ahero Evangelical School of Theology (AEST) class huddling together in the front corner of the sanctuary. Laughter met him as he approached.

"Hello, Pastor Benard," a young man greeted him. The others turned and followed his lead, some still awkward around the head teacher with classes having started only a month ago. The students adored Benard and most chatted easily with him. His genuineness drew them.

Benard greeted them with his shining smile. "Good morning! How is everybody today?" He loved the students and relished the opportunity to participate in their learning process. If only he had more time to spend with them. Already, he had written the entire curriculum for the 1993-94 school year and had spent countless hours preparing for the eighteen students accepted into the upcoming class. But all this had begun to take a serious toll on his commitment to support church plants. With Pamela's time nearing, he knew his schedule would become even more restricted. For now, however, he was determined to enjoy the students for as long as God gave him in this blessed place.

Benard passed his squirming eighteen-month-old baby, Betha, to Pamela before rising to preach the Sunday sermon.

"Good morning, brothers and sisters in Christ." He welcomed newcomers and then said, "I have an announcement to make concerning the Ahero Evangelical School of Theology. For two years, I have tried to help run the school, write curriculum, and attend to my support duties as a church planter.

"Due to increasing enrollment—we praise the Lord for the

twenty-eight students starting next week—and my growing family, I feel I can no longer continue to perform all of these functions. After much prayer and discussion, Mama Pamela and I have decided to permanently relocate to Ahero in order to devote our full attention to local ministries."

Applause broke out. Some whooped and hollered as Benard locked eyes with Pamela. What a wonderful thing, to feel so wanted.

"Thank you, friends. We look forward to serving alongside you full-time."

Ahero Evangelical School of Theology (AEST)

Seminary students studying outside

Chapter Nine

Friends of Christ

R ain drizzled from the sky. The worst of the storm had passed, but for one, Pamela knew it had only just begun. She and Benard sat on the sofa with a weeping mother of three. For the past two hours, they had held her hands and listened as she unburdened her troubled, mourning heart.

Her husband had died from exhaustion and malnutrition only four days ago, and now, she had no food for her family. Despair darkened her usually lovely countenance, and she clung to Benard and Pamela like a candle in a cave, unwilling to let go of the hope they held within them.

"I can't believe he is gone," she lamented with a faraway look in her reddening eyes. "It hurts so much!" The young widow clenched a fist and pulled it to her chest as her breath came in short gasps. "He made everything right even though we had nothing, and he worked so hard for us—so hard that it killed him."

Glassy-eyed children sat on the floor, unmoved by the sound of their mother's now-familiar sobs.

"Look, look at them," she wailed, motioning towards the floor. "These children have no father. No father . . ."

Pamela drew the woman into her arms and stroked her hair tenderly. "You are not alone, my sister. We will help you and the children through this time." Pamela moved so she could see the widow's pained face. "You must believe that God will never leave you. He knows your pain and will help you bear it." Her voice quieted. "You must care for your little ones, too, Mama. They need you now."

Her words stilled the young mother who slowly nodded, straightened, and wiped her tears with a small blue rag.

"You're right, Mama Pamela. Oh my! What time is it? You've been here so long. I must send you on your way. Thank you. Thank you both for coming."

Pastor Benard prayed for the family and then brought in a box of foodstuffs from the car.

"This should keep you for the week, Mama. I wish it was more, but we will do our best to look after you all. Please, never feel alone."

He pointed to the leaking roof in the corner. "I will bring tools to fix that on Tuesday, and maybe Mama Pamela can find a couple of bottles of clean drinking water to send with me."

Pamela nodded. "We love you all so much, Mama." The women embraced as Benard offered a kind smile.

"You are in our prayers, Mama. God bless you," Benard said, giving the children vigorous hugs and receiving smiles from all of them. The kids clung to him, hungry for the fatherly affection life demanded they learn to live without. He handed the littlest one into his mother's arms and again promised to return the following week. Pamela gave her one more hug.

"Mama, Mama! Can we eat? What did they bring us?" Famished children reached into the mysterious box and cried with glee over the cornmeal, fruit, and lentils.

"I will feed you now, my children."

Pamela saw the widow smile and guessed it might be the first time in weeks, for she knew that nothing made a mother hurt worse than not being able to feed her children. Things had seemed tight for Pamela and Benard when Melissa, now three years old, had come along. And then baby Dorothy had been born, but the Lord had always provided.

"Go wash your hands while I prepare dinner," the widow said.

They scurried away as Pamela saw tears slip unbidden down the young widow's cheeks.

"May God bless you both for your great kindness to us."

Pamela was quiet. Benard eyed her with suspicion, wondering where her mind had run.

"Everything okay?" Only when she turned her head did he see her tears.

"Benard, there are so many like her," Pamela said. "So many widows without food, without hope."

Pamela was incredible. Just when he thought he couldn't love her more, she would say something like that. Her compassion moved him deeply.

"I know, Pamela, my love. The list of widows continues to grow as does the number of orphans."

Reports of children losing parents to AIDS and malnutrition flooded his world daily, and his biggest problem had quickly become not being able to care for all of them. These precious souls had no one on earth to fight for them, to feed them, to protect them . . . His heart broke, and he yearned to do more.

Please show us what to do, Lord.

Benard's mother relished the surprise visit from her youngest son. Her heart had flip-flopped when he appeared in the doorway even though she immediately sensed something troubled him.

"Come, Benard, sit by me."

She waited and wondered. He must have finished surveying the homes of Wachara widows. Perhaps that was why he appeared upset.

Sweet Benard had a big heart. She and Papa had Benard to thank for their relationships with God. He had come home after completing Kapsabet Bible College and led both of them to Christ as well as two of her children. Her three living children maintained a staunch, Seventh-day Adventist faith as did many others in the village.

Benard continually challenged them. "How can you call yourselves Christians and yet believe Jesus is the Son of God without power?

Keeping the Sabbath will not save you," Benard would argue. "Only faith in Jesus Christ can truly save."

After many discussions, Benard obviously realized talk was futile. She knew he dreamed of one day planting an evangelical church in Wachara so that the tribe could see faith lived out on a day-to-day basis, but for now, ancient rituals and cultural beliefs inhibited them from seeing the Truth or their need for it.

Mama frowned. Perhaps the new widow had been inherited by her brother-in-law. Tribal elders usually insisted that widows remarry their husband's closest male relative according to tradition. Benard had tried multiple times to dissuade them from this practice.

"Look at how the men use widows for food and sex," Benard argued. "These inheritance arrangements do not produce fathers who care for the widow's children or give her emotional and financial support. They destroy families."

The elders defended their practice by quoting the story of Ruth, a woman inherited by a distant relative. Benard defended his position with the New Testament. "But that happened hundreds of years before Christ came. You do not accept the power He has to change the world; therefore, you refuse to understand that it is better for a widow to live alone if she chooses."

"Have some hot milk, Benard," Mama said. She poured the warm, chalky beverage into a chipped brown mug and placed it in front of him.

"Thank you, Mama." He sipped twice and then allowed his heartache to spill from his lips. "Mama, I visit the villages and see the lives of the people," he said, his voice raw with emotion. "Every time, I cry." He wiped his eyes. "I go to widows' homes and see that they live in leaking houses without food and proper water. The children are hungry, and they have no one to provide for them. Who will fight for them, Mama? I get so frustrated!"

Seeming unable to sit any longer, he rose and paced the small living area of his parents' home.

Solemnly his mother nodded. "Your father is the oldest of our tribesmen, Benard. Many men of the village have died, and three-quarters of the women are widows, most with children to feed. Some of the mothers have died because they have to work so hard after their husbands are gone."

She paused, not wanting to add to his troubled heart but knowing he needed the truth. "We struggle to care for the village orphans, Benard. Times are difficult."

God had bestowed a generous portion of the gift of mercy on her son, and she knew it to be both a blessing and a burden for him. Her mother's heart wanted to ease the pain, but her faith in Christ helped her believe that God had a reason for intimately involving Benard in the suffering of the people

But for what purpose, Lord?

"Pamela and I have been talking and praying," he said. "We cannot bear to watch the orphans and widows suffer as they do. Plans are underway to start a ministry called Friends of Christ to help meet the needs of orphans and widows in Ahero and Wachara."

Mama's heart stirred with excitement. "Tell me more, my son."

He gulped the last of his milk and wiped his mouth.

"The plan in Ahero is to open a small orphanage school in 2000 with enough space for 48 children. We have hired a teacher, prepared the building and curriculum, and acquired enough porridge to feed them once each day for a month.

"This will relieve the foster families of providing lunch for their children five days a week. The children will receive spiritual nourishment as well as the education they need to make a better life for themselves."

"Will the children live at the school?" she asked.

"No, Mama. They will live with foster families and come to the school during the day. I am sad to say that . . ." He paused to regain control. "Plenty of orphans want to come to the school. We cannot take all of them." He shifted in his seat.

"The visits we've taken to homes where widows as well as people with HIV and AIDS live have opened doors for us to tell families about Friends of Christ. We have not been able to get enough money to give them food, but we try to help buy medicines and teach them how to keep their homes and bodies clean.

"Most of all, the visits help us stay on top of the children. We connect them with foster parents who will look after them when they're not in school and become a family to them. Once their parents die from AIDS, the kids often drop out of school and have no money, no shoes, nowhere to live . . . That's why we must do this, Mama. We must."

Proud tears filled his mother's eyes.

"Benard, I will pray for you and Pamela. This is a good thing you want to do for the people. Our God will bring it to pass and bless it."

2000

Benard and Pamela stood all smiles as cheers erupted from the small cluster of people gathered in front of a tiny two-room building. Inside, crude desks and benches made up the classroom for the spanking new Friends of Christ Orphanage in Ahero. Benard had already selected twenty-seven children for the first class.

All of them lived with guardians or relatives who provided places to sleep while the school provided food and education during the week. It was a modest beginning, and everyone looked forward to expanding the program in the future.

For now, Benard raised his hands and turned to the people. "Let us pray and thank the Lord for answering our prayer."

Friends of Christ Orphanage, Ahero

Chapter Ten

Street Boys

Benard eyed the eight-year-old forking over precious coins to a shoe repair salesman. Checking over his shoulder, the older man handed the boy a small container. The youngster's eyes widened with delight as he beheld his precious treasure.

Not another one. Benard shook his head and continued walking. Glue. The huffing addiction enslaved most of the boys living on the Kisumu streets. Cheaper than food and shelter, glue offered benefits at an affordable price. Kids used it to suppress their appetites, keep warm in the chilly air, and give them a powerful high.

Life on the streets could be cruel. Benard's heart broke every time he came here. He must do something. He had collected the items on Pamela's shopping list within twenty minutes and hurried down to the worst section of town to see if he could find some boys he could help.

For the children whose parents or relatives abused them, kicked them out due to lack of food, or simply didn't want them anymore, the street held hope for a better life. Benard knew that in other countries like America, many teens joined gangs in order to feel a sense of belonging and family. So, too, Kenyan children, ranging in age from five to thirty, searched for acceptance, food, and shelter on the street when they faced rejection at home.

Benard thought about the young girl with AIDS he had prayed with in the hospital right before she died. Poor child. Dead and nobody cared. After her parents died, she dropped out of school and turned to prostitution. As the oldest child in the home, the girl had five siblings depending on her every day for food, shelter, and affection. The fourteen-year-old struggled to make ends meet all by herself, and the stress of it all coupled with AIDS had driven her to the grave. Benard had later found her siblings lying naked and alone in the house, too weakened by the demons of starvation to answer the door.

Her story compared with that of many young women in Kisumu. Girls actually seemed to fare better financially than boys until HIV destroyed their health. Orphaned boys relied on begging and stealing for their income, and sometimes, the older street boys put the younger ones to "work," demanding a cut of their profits in exchange for protection while doing business.

Boy after boy approached Benard and begged him for money. Each time he shook his head. "I have no money, Son, but I would like to help you." Empty, glazed eyes stared back at him. Benard knew that years of huffing could cause brain damage, but most of the kids he encountered were still enjoying their morning high. None accepted his offer. They simply wandered off, looking to find the next approachable person.

Benard knew that bringing boys such as these back to the orphanage would not help them. The orphanage could not provide the specific attention they would need in order to fully recover from their addictions. Today, he looked for the boys who had not yet become glue addicts—the ones who lingered in that in-between, vulnerable place of realization that the street held no hope for them.

I will find you, he vowed. *I know more of you are out there, and I want with all my heart to help you, to give you a home and a family, to make you feel loved and accepted.* He sighed and began the trek back up to the car. It would be dark soon.

Frustrated by his time constraints, the lack of pastors to help with this ministry, and the children cold and alone on the streets of Kisumu, Benard wiped his eyes.

I wish I could take all of you home and be a father to you.

Part Two

Vision

Where there is no vision, the people perish.

Proverbs 29:18 (KJV)

Chapter Eleven

The Answer

Widows. Orphans. Homeless children. Children who want to go to school but can't afford uniforms. Men who work too hard and starve to death. Girls who sell their bodies in order to eat and provide for their families. Students who want to learn but cannot afford an education. Pastors who are overworked and burnt out because they try to help so many. Boys who sniff glue. Parents who have contracted AIDS. Families who need health care . . .

Benard lay with his face to the floor.

O God, O God! When will it end? He sobbed uncontrollably, his face contorted. The pain of the people tormented him day and night, and the depths of his compassionate spirit felt each burden as his own.

What can I do? I know that You love them all, that You see their pain. I want to help them, Father. Please, show me how I can help them. I cannot bear to stand by and watch so much suffering in this place! I must do something, something more.

Please, Father, Benard sobbed, his tears soaking the straw mat beneath him. *Allow me to help them. Use me to touch them with Your love, to tell them about the hope they can have in Your Son, Jesus Christ. Deliver us from this vicious cycle and save this community that is desperate, dying, and without hope.*

Show me, Lord, Benard pleaded. *I will do whatever You want.*

"Pamela! Pamela! Where are you?" Benard rushed into the kitchen of his Ahero home to find his surprised wife staring at him over a mound of dirty dishes.

"Benard, I thought you were praying—"

"I was, but I am done now." He took her wet hand and pulled her away from the sink. "I have to tell you what the Lord has given me!"

Pamela finished drying her hands. *What on earth?* She'd never seen Benard like this before. She waited in silence for him to share his revelation as she folded the brown kitchen towel. Like rising bread dough, she felt her excitement growing.

This must be good.

Benard pressed a closed fist to his trembling lips. Light seemed to pour from his body and illuminate the small, dark room. He turned toward her, and she saw tears gathering in his eyes.

"Oh Pamela, God has given me a tremendous vision for our people! I need to find thirty acres of land so that we can build foster homes and classrooms, a recreation center, a worship chapel, and a hospital!"

Pamela stared at him in awe. "What? That's incredible, but Benard, you must slow down—"

"I'm sorry, Pamela. I am overcome!" His face shone as he paced the tiny room. "I pray that in twenty years I am still alive to see all that God has revealed come to pass. Oh, Pamela!" He grabbed her hands and whirled her around the room.

She giggled with delight, thrilled to be a part of this wonderful moment.

"You know what else? We will keep cows for milk, plant vegetables, and try to build a fish pond to show the children how to be responsible. We should teach them how to live, starting by keeping chickens, keeping cows, keeping fish, and showing them that we don't have to buy, buy, buy. We can eat what is there for us."

Tingles raced up and down Pamela's spine. "Benard, these ideas are wonderful!"

Her encouragement spurred him on.

"If we can place five to ten orphans in each of the twelve homes with a foster mother or father, we can provide them with parental love. Meeting their physical needs is not enough. Without parental love, we are torturing them psychologically. We need someone to come and tell them, 'You are my child. I have accepted you in my home, and we can do things together. You are valuable. You can go to school. You have access to education, and when you are sick, you can go to the health center and be treated. God created you in His own image. You matter greatly to God.'"

"Oh, Benard." Her voice shook. "That is a beautiful vision."

He sat next to her on the bed and took her hand, his face suddenly serious.

"The other thing God showed me is that I must go back to school, Pamela. I need more education in order to better train more pastors at AEST. The Lord will provide financially as He always has—I'm certain of that. I'm not sure where to go . . . maybe the United States . . . but the sooner I start, the sooner I can finish and begin these projects."

The full impact hit her like the trunk of a mother elephant protecting her young. He was going away to school, and when he got back, he would be busier than ever. She thought about how his time spent away from home had already increased drastically over the past few years. Seeing him even less would be hard for the children . . . and for her . . .

But look at him. His eyes glistened, and confidence poured from his being. She knew Benard and knew well that God had used him greatly to touch the lives of thousands. *Who am I to say anything against the will of God? I must know my place and support my husband in doing all that the Lord tells him.*

"So tell me, Pamela, what do you think? About everything?"

She smiled. "I'd better help you pack your bag."

Part Three

Called

*I urge you to live a life worthy of the calling
you have received.*

Ephesians 4:1

Chapter Twelve

Columbia International University

AUGUST, 2001

What was he doing? Benard leaned back in his seat as the aircraft sped down the runway headed for New York City. He had almost missed his Amsterdam connection, and the predicted turbulence ahead made this first-time flyer nervous. When the plane landed, he would still need to travel the last leg of his journey to Columbia International University (CIU) in a place called South Carolina.

He stared out the window and noticed that the sky had darkened. Pamela's face flashed before him, unbidden. She had bravely seen him off, giving him the last $40 they had in this world.

"You will need it, Benard," she insisted as she pressed the money into his hand.

He missed dear Pamela already.

Tears came to his eyes as he thought of her and their children. He bowed his head, holding the crumpled bills in his hand. *O God, how am I going to be away from them?* He thought of one-year-old little Dorothy. He didn't even really know her yet. *Will she even remember me?*

The left wing of the plane dipped, then the right. Benard gripped his armrests and searched the faces of his fellow passengers. Across the aisle, a well-dressed businessman typing on a laptop seemed annoyed but unafraid. Calmed, Benard returned to his thoughts.

Lord, help me to have faith in Your plan for my life.

Benard knew God had called him to go to CIU because of the miracles that took place before his departure. His burden for training pastors had deepened in its intensity. Missionaries from CIU had visited Kenya and encouraged Benard to consider attending CIU, a school with an emphasis on missions and intercultural studies. Even though they would not accept all of his credits from Kapsabet Bible College, CIU had developed a personalized four-year plan for him to earn both his Bachelor's Degree and a Master's of Theology. Private donations, church support, and a promise for sponsorship from an uncle had propelled Benard to purchase a plane ticket and arrange on-campus living arrangements.

Everything had fallen into place perfectly until . . .

"Benard, I know this is a bad time because you are leaving next month." Benard's brother shoved his hands in his pockets and avoided eye contact with Benard and Pamela as they sat in the muggy living room.

"I don't know how to . . . uh, tell you." He paused. "Our uncle passed away last evening."

Pamela drew a deep breath while Benard sat on the sofa, stunned. *How could this happen now?* Benard tried to take it all in.

"How is everybody doing?"

With eyes full of regret, his brother spoke. "Okay . . . but Benard, you will not get the money he promised you for school. The family has to use it for the burial." His brother swallowed. "I am sorry, Benard. I know how much you wanted to go to school."

Having delivered his message, the somber brother headed back to Wachara, declining the offer to spend the night. Secretly, Benard was thankful. His heart felt heavy, and he needed to pray.

God, are You closing the door? It had all seemed so right. He was certain . . . had been certain. He wrestled for hours and lost track of the time he spent on his knees weeping and praying.

Pamela knocked. After a minute, the door opened. "Benard, we will continue to pray about this, but if you still believe God wants you to go, you should go. He would never lead you to a place where He cannot provide for you."

She was so wise.

"You are right, Pamela. Thank you." He held out his hand. "Will you pray with me?"

Benard pulled down the tray from the back of the seat in front of him and folded his hands. You want to increase my trust in You, Lord. He had only forty American dollars, and CIU needed $3500 for the semester.

O God, please help me trust You to provide the money for me to go to school. Lead me to many Americans You will raise up to help my people, and help me to believe in You and Your provision for all my needs and for Pamela and the kids, too, that You will take care of them while I am away.

He stared out the window. Four years seemed like an eternity.

Who was that guy? Intercultural Studies major Teri Miles spotted the beaming African across the room at CIU's 2001 Freshman Orientation. His booming voice, charming accent, and friendly manner had drawn a small cluster of students. After several minutes, the crowd cleared and Teri made his way over.

"Hi there, I'm Teri Miles. Are you a transfer student?"

"Hello, Teri. I'm Benard. Benard Ondiek. I am so happy to meet you."

The man was all smiles.

"Yes, I am a transfer student from Kapsabet Bible College in Nairobi, Kenya."

"Wow, you've come a long way," Teri said. *Talk about dedication.* "What brought you all the way to CIU?"

"I am a pastor, and I want to help my people by training more pastors. In order to do this, I must have more education. Some missionaries told me that CIU would be a good place to learn because it puts a great emphasis on missions and also strives to meet the needs of international students."

Teri nodded. "Yes, CIU's focus on missions attracted me too. I've been on overseas missions trips in the past and really wanted a program that would prepare me for potential full-time ministry."

Benard grinned. "That is wonderful, Teri." He motioned to two chairs at a nearby table. "Why don't you tell me about your family?"

Teri chatted easily with his new friend for the next hour and found him pleasant and thoughtful, humble and unafraid to share things most Americans kept hidden behind a mask.

"Did I hear you right, Pastor Benard? You're married?"

"Yes, I am, to a wonderful woman named Pamela." His face glowed as he raved about her. "And I have four children—Abraham, Betha, Melissa, and Dorothy."

Pastor Benard's reality hit Teri like a ton of bricks. *This man is telling me that he is going to spend the next four years away from his family because he needs education to train more pastors for ministry!* Teri gulped. *Talk about sacrifice!*

The pastor seemed to sense the impact his words had on his new, blonde-haired friend.

"I am here out of obedience, Teri. It is the hardest thing I have ever done. My family has sacrificed so much for the ministry . . ." His voice broke, but he regained his composure and spoke with confidence. "I miss them already, but I know the Lord wants me here."

What was that noise? Pamela froze. Her heart thundered, and she suddenly felt like thousands of mosquitoes pricked her skin simultaneously. She heard glass and metal clanking in the living room. *O God, protect us from these bandits!*

Pastor Wilson had returned to Nairobi to work as a Bible translator, and the group of pastors he had left behind turned on Pamela as soon as Benard went to CIU. In spite of the fact that Benard had entrusted his family to this group of pastors prior to leaving, they refused to help Pamela pay the rent and basically abandoned her. Two weeks later, the landlord had evicted her, and she and the children scavenged for food and shelter, moving from place to place.

Her heart broke when her children stared up at her this evening with big hungry eyes. *What do I feed them, Lord? Where should we go?*

A church member had told Pamela that the owner of this shack had abandoned it three months ago, and in desperation, Pamela had brought her children to this place.

More banging and rummaging. *Maybe they will not find us,* she tried to convince herself. She had purposefully chosen this spot in the darkest recesses of the small tin dwelling to hide both her family and their belongings. The front of the house still appeared empty. Her children huddled around her, the warmth of her body their only comfort in this dark, hungry place. *O Lord, keep them asleep that they may not know my great fear.*

Male voices pierced the night. She clutched little Dorothy closer. *O God, please protect us!*

What was Teacher saying? Benard rifled through his papers frantically. *Where was the good professor reading from? He could not possibly be speaking English.* Benard fought back tears. *Only the first day of class and I'm lost already.* Dr. Layman droned on, oblivious to Benard's frantic plight.

"And we will wrap up the semester with a preview of next semester's material. Western Civilization is one of the more challenging classes we offer here at CIU, and I hope you will get a lot out of the course. If you would please turn to page twelve in your textbooks, you will see . . ."

Benard opened his book and found page twelve. Good. Progress. As he read page twelve with the class, his heart sank as he realized that he could speak English much better than he could read it. His two semester-long English courses at Kapsabet Bible College seemed distant and unhelpful at the moment. The words swam underneath his watery eyes. He was in big trouble. He bent over his desk and furrowed his brow, mouthing the words to each sentence.

"That will be all for today, everybody. Be sure to read chapter one tonight. See you tomorrow!"

The whole chapter? Benard flipped to the end of chapter one. *Thirty-four pages.* He gulped. *I'm a dead man.*

Four desks over, an astute classmate had observed the dark-skinned, smiling Kenyan from the moment he walked in the room. He had a presence about him. Throughout the class, she couldn't help but notice how he struggled to understand the teacher's lecture. She wondered how much English he knew. Western Civ. was challenging enough without throwing a language barrier into the mix.

Rising, she gathered her notebook and text. Maybe he could use a little help—and a friend. The spunky blonde headed for her classmate who now poured over his assignment. Watching for a moment, her heart broke for him. She chose to interrupt his thoughts.

"Good morning, there. I'm Laura Wollenhaupt," she said and stuck out her hand. "What's your name?"

Startled, Benard recovered and stood. "Hello, Laura. I'm Pastor Benard."

Never one to beat-around-the-bush, she said, "Pastor Benard, this class is very difficult. Do you understand what Dr. Layman is saying?"

He looked down and shook his head. "It is very hard."

She took a step closer to him. "I'm going to help you, Pastor Benard."

His face lit up. "Really, Laura? I think I will need a lot of help."

She grinned. "Believe me, Pastor Benard. The honor is mine."

Chapter Thirteen

Chicken Nugget Night

"Whew, that quiz was tough!" Teri shook his head. He followed Laura and Benard into the hallway, turning to talk to Genevieve Ferrin and Chris Matthews.

Laura pulled Benard aside and whispered, "Pastor Benard, how did you do?"

His grin showed all of his teeth. "I passed it."

Laura jumped up and down, cheering. "What did you get?"

Benard knew Laura would be happy for him. "I got a B+!"

She raised her arms over her head and hollered. "Wahoo!" Placing a hand on his shoulder, she said, "Pastor Benard, you've worked so hard. You are so good!"

"What's going on over here?" Teri and his two friends walked up.

Benard's smile froze. *Let me see. I think they are called Chris and ... something long. Please help me, Lord.*

"Hey, Genevieve, are you going to practice tonight?" Chris stood ready with his guitar. "If not, I'll drop this off at the dorm."

That's it! Genevieve. Thank You!

"Benard, please don't worry about us. We'll be fine." Pamela clutched the receiver, regretting she had asked for advice about what to do. She should have known it would worry him. From now on, she would figure things out. Pamela was convinced that God had called Benard to CIU, and as hard as it was to live without him physically by her side, she knew remaining steadfast in her faith was the best way to support him. "God is taking care of us, remember?"

Silence. Pamela waited, fearing that the little she had admitted would undo her husband.

"Pamela, what are you going to do? I feel so frustrated. I hate being so far away from you and the children." He sighed. "I cannot believe the landlord kicked you out and that the pastors . . ." Benard wept.

Pamela scrambled to find something positive to say. "Benard, we know the Lord called you to CIU, right?"

"Right."

"Then we must believe He will take care of us—you at CIU and me at home with the children." She wiped her eyes and steadied her voice. "We must have faith."

"But what will you do?" His question echoed her fears.

"The Lord knows, Benard," she said, drawing strength from the words. "The Lord knows."

Benard felt blessed to have made so many new friends at CIU, especially Laura. With her fine tutoring, he actually found himself enjoying Western Civ. Not only was she an excellent tutor, she also had become a good friend. They spent many hours together, and she soaked up everything he shared about his family, ministry, and life.

Teri had also proven to be a faithful friend.

"Hey, Pastor Benard," he asked while clasping a hand on Benard's shoulder one early November day, "what are you doing for Thanksgiving?"

Teri was one thoughtful person.

Benard actually had dreaded the departure of his friends and wondered what he would do without them for an entire week. *Dare he hope?* "I have no plans," he said.

"Good!" Teri grinned. "Then you can come home with me! You can meet my family and sample Mom's good cooking."

"Thank you, my friend." Benard's voice dripped with emotion. His first Thanksgiving in the United States would be spent with a real friend. "Thank you."

"Things are better, Benard—really." Pamela hoped he believed her. Things were better, but still difficult. A neighbor had taken pity on her and had given her some chickens. At least now the children had food again, and they had a steady income from the eggs she sold at the market. Pamela's asthma had flared up from all of the stress, but the Lord continued to sustain her through these terrible times.

"Oh, what a relief, Pamela!" He mumbled a prayer of thanks. "I was going to come home."

She could hear him relax. Smiling, she fingered the buttons on the phone. "I told you the Lord would provide." She did not tell him about the continued safety issues, the lack of food for herself, and the lack of funds for the children's school clothes. There were many things she would never tell him.

He must finish school.

"So, Pastor Benard, does the Miles family get you for Christmas this year?"

Benard smiled. "Thank you, Teri, but a friend has invited me to Michigan." He paused. "Teri, is it very cold in Michigan?"

Teri grinned and nodded. "Yes, indeed. Maybe you'll even get to see some snow!"

"Snow! I have seen pictures of snow in books," Benard said, clapping his hands together. "It looks so beautiful."

Teri laughed. "You'll get to see for yourself."

By the time Benard returned to CIU after Christmas, he determined that he had seen enough snow. Michigan was now the coldest place he had ever been and ever wanted to be. Brrr!

Before leaving for the break, Teri had helped Benard move his few belongings from on-campus housing to a small rental house on the edge of campus. Now he walked Benard home from the train. The house stood stone cold upon their arrival. Teri stared at his shivering companion.

"Pastor Benard, didn't you leave the heat on while you left for break?"

Benard shot him a puzzled look. *You could turn heat on?*

"No, I don't know what you're talking about," he said.

Realization washed over Teri in one big wave. "Oh, of course not! Wow, I didn't even think of that! Aw, man . . . here." Teri made his way to the thermostat. "Let me show you."

"Hello, Pamela."

"Benard, why did you send for me to call you? Is everything okay?" Pamela had hurried to town, fearing the worst.

"Yes, Pamela, everything is fine."

She could picture his wide smile. Only then did she relax after the many long hours before his call. "Thank the Lord."

"I have good news. I have gotten a job cleaning the library and will send money home to you and the children." He paused. "It won't be much, but it will help some."

"Thank you, Benard!" Now she could plant sugarcane and corn and buy fabric for dresses to sell at the market! She felt a weight lift off her back. "Are you sure it won't interfere with your studies?"

"Pamela, thoughts of my family are what interfere with my studies. I will feel better doing something to provide for my family."

"How are you doing, Benard?"

"The classes are going okay now that Laura is helping me with English and Melissa is helping me with math. And I am making friends. Lots of friends."

She cringed. "But?"

"I don't know how I am going to pay for school . . . The school is being patient with me, but I don't know what to do. Soon, they will be forced to kick me out if I cannot pay." He paused. "Pamela, I'm struggling . . . struggling to have faith."

"Benard, if you have no faith now, how will you come home and tell the people to have faith?" Pamela sensed the powerful battle looming over her husband's spirit, and she prayed for his protection.

"Benard, you must ask God to give you faith."

"Hey, Pastor Benard, is it still okay for us to come over tonight?" Genevieve asked. "Chris and I will bring our guitars."

"Wonderful!" Benard beamed. How lovely it would be in his house tonight with all of his friends! "Yes, I want all of you to come tonight and share my new house with me." Living in the dorm had limited Benard's ability to entertain guests, something that was as much a part of him as his broad, toothy grin and contagious joy. How could they possibly know how much he had looked forward to tonight?

"We'll see you tonight then, Pastor Benard! And do not eat dinner. We'll bring you chicken nuggets!"

About six o'clock that night, Chris slammed the lid of Teri's trunk and headed around to the passenger seat, sliding inside.

"All set, Captain Miles. Ready for takeoff."

Laura and Genevieve giggled from the backseat as Teri coerced his bucket of bolts to transport the gang to McDonald's. The odor of frying oil wafted its way into the car as they ordered five boxes of chicken nuggets.

"Chicken nuggets are my absolute favorite," Laura declared.

"It's a good thing," Chris said. "We've got plenty of them."

"I'm so excited to hang out with Pastor Benard!" Laura said, practically bouncing up and down.

Chris agreed. Pastor Benard had to be the friendliest guy he had ever met. The presence of tangible joy on his face amazed and drew everyone. Even in the midst of the difficult financial circumstances that threatened his educational career, Pastor Benard clung to the Lord and remained positive.

"Here we are," Teri announced. He pulled into a parking spot and shut off the engine. Like a swarm of bees eager to pollinate, the group hurried from the car to the white clapboard house.

Pastor Benard was waiting for them.

"Come in, my friends! Come in!" He waved them in, hugging each one and taking their coats. His home bore worn, sparse furnishings but was immaculate. He had pulled a table close to the sofas and nestled the only chairs in the house around it. Chris and Genevieve plopped their guitar cases onto the living room floor as Laura held up her white paper bag with glee.

"We brought lots of chicken nuggets!"

"Wonderful, let's ask the Lord to bless our food," Pastor Benard said, bowing his head.

His sincere gratitude humbled them, forever endearing him to this eclectic group.

He didn't want them to go.

"Thanks again, Pastor Benard! We had a wonderful time!" Benard's friends stood bundled and ready by the front door.

"Please, everyone, let's do this again next Sunday!"

"Are you sure?" Laura asked. "That would be spectacular!"

"Yes, I want you to come. I want all of you to come again." He paused for emphasis. "With chicken nuggets."

Everyone laughed and nodded enthusiastically. Benard took his time saying goodbye, hugging his guests and then waving as they drove away. When he shut the door, the house seemed strangely quiet. He was glad his roommate would be home soon.

All traces of his houseguests vanished in less than two minutes as he rearranged the tables and chairs. What beautiful songs they had sung! God's Spirit rested upon this place and had spoken to them while they prayed. Benard turned off the light and headed for his bedroom. Chris and Genevieve played the guitar so well. How extraordinary to worship the Lord with such music!

He hummed a few bars of his favorite tune on the way to his

room. After removing his shoes, Benard checked the time. Every other Sunday evening, Pamela tried to call him from the store in town. If he needed to talk to her, he would call the store and ask for someone to send a message to Pamela.

He would have to wait to take a shower.

The ringing phone startled him. He drank in the sound of his wife's lovely voice. She updated him on the Friends of Christ Orphanage and other happenings.

He could not wait to go home for the summer and see everything—and everyone—himself.

Sunday after Sunday, the foursome purchased a slew of chicken nuggets and made their way to the home of their teacher and friend. They had naturally become interested in his life and ministry as they had gotten to know him, and the more they learned about him, the more they loved him.

"You know, Pastor Benard," Laura commented to him one Sunday night, "you've become a surrogate father to all of us. God has used you to teach us so many things."

"I praise Him for that, Laura." He sighed. "It is a miracle I am here with my financial situation . . . and my loneliness."

Pamela would call later tonight from the store, encouraging him to stay strong in the Lord. She always knew exactly when he needed it most. She knew him so well. How he missed her—and the children. He shook off his reverie.

"Maybe we should have a time of prayer now. Does anybody have a need?"

"I do," Laura said. "You all know my friend, Lexi. Well, she has suffered from a scratching disorder called Lichen's Disease for the past thirteen years." Tears spilled down Laura's cheeks. "She has small scabs on her ankles and sometimes other places that bother her continually." Her voice broke. "I would simply like for us to pray for her healing."

"Of course." Benard's eyes watered.

"She hasn't told anyone outside of family before, but she gave me permission to share it with you tonight."

"Let us boldly approach the Throne," Benard said.

Pamela couldn't believe it. In less than a week, Benard would be home for the summer. She could hardly think about anything else but forced herself to tidy the small room with the leak in the back corner floor. She smiled. *Benard will fix it.*

Scanning the mats with sleeping children, she shuddered to think about how they had almost been forced to live on the street. Benard could now come back to a home and see his children eating and happy. *Thank You, Father. Thank You for watching over us, Lord. Please bring Benard home safely.*

Benard leaned his head against the window of the 737, closing his eyes and sighing. The summer had gone too quickly, and now he had nine months ahead without the kids.

And Pamela. Sweet Pamela. He missed her already. Seeing her in the deplorable abandoned shack without running water and electricity sickened him. How could he have left them behind? What kind of man does such a thing?

He had thought the pastors would watch over his precious family, but the betrayal proved worse than anything Benard could have imagined. Thanks to God, Pamela and the children had survived. Knowing this eased the daunting task of forgiving the pastors, but the wound left behind would take time to heal.

Shaking his head, he thanked God that his children had respected him upon his arrival home. Pamela had done an excellent job with them, and he quietly slipped back into the family, letting her continue to carry out her regular routine.

Benard thought about the Friends of Christ Orphanage, filled with smiling children in pink and blue uniforms. His visits to that place made his time at CIU seem like an eternity.

O God, he prayed, *please strengthen me for another year.*

Chapter Fourteen

Culture Shock

THANKSGIVING 2002

W e're home!" Laura bounded through the front doorway of her parents' Pennsylvania home, dragging a suddenly shy Benard by the arm. He stared at the big restored barn. Like they said in America—Wow!

"Come on, Pastor Benard! I want you to meet my family." She turned just as her mother made her way down the stairs.

"Welcome home, Laura." They embraced, giggled, and turned to Benard, keeping their arms comfortably around each other. Laura grinned at Benard.

"Mom, I want you to meet Pastor Benard Ondiek of Ahero, Kenya."

Benard moved closer to shake her hand.

"I'm pleased to meet you, Pastor Benard," Laura's mother said with deep kindness in her eyes. "Please call me Sue."

She seemed to have the same spirit as Laura. Warmth and sincerity radiated from her greeting and made him feel truly welcome in their home. He could tell this was the mother of his friend.

"Oh, Mama Sue!" He gave Mama Sue a big hug. "I am happy to meet Laura's mother."

Mama Sue laughed.

She has so much joy flowing from her, Benard thought. *It makes her laugh into a most beautiful sound.*

"I'm sorry Greg isn't here to meet you as well." She checked her watch. "He should be home any minute, but Amy and David are—"

"Right behind you, Mom," said Amy, lurking in the kitchen doorway with David. Laura rushed to hug them and introduced Pastor Benard.

"Amy, David." As Benard hugged them, he thought of his own children back in Ahero. How he missed them. Laura's voice bounced into his thoughts.

"Smells like dinner's almost ready. What did you make, Mom?"

Mama Sue looked surprised. "Chicken nuggets, of course."

"You're awesome, Mom!" Laura cheered.

"Hi, everybody!" Pastor Greg strode through a different doorway than the one Benard and Laura had entered.

Benard peered into the garage. How did Papa Greg come in like that? He would ask him later.

Laura ran to Papa Greg and threw herself into his arms. "Hi, Dad!"

Benard scanned the circle of Wollenhaupts. What a nice family. He was blessed to be in such a place of love for Thanksgiving.

Laura swept a hand dramatically toward Benard. "Pastor Benard Ondiek, meet my father, Pastor Greg Wollenhaupt."

"Pastor Greg, it is so nice to meet you. Laura has told me many things about you. You and Mama Sue have a wonderful daughter." He motioned towards Amy and David. "Three wonderful children."

"Well, thank you, Pastor Benard." Pastor Greg smiled wide. "I hear you have a houseful of your own. Four children, right?"

Benard nodded. "I am blessed!"

"I'll say!" Pastor Greg made his way over to kiss Mama Sue. "Hi, Sweetheart. Is dinner ready?"

Mama Sue snapped into action mode. "It sure is. Amy, would you help me please?"

"Sure, Mom."

"Why don't you have a seat, Pastor Benard?" Pastor Greg pulled out the end seat for him.

Grateful, Benard sank into it, not only hungry but also tired from the eleven-hour drive.

Pastor Greg chatted comfortably while they waited. "After dinner we'll go to the Thanksgiving Eve service at church. Laura's been dying to introduce you to her church family."

Benard's weariness melted away. "I will be happy to meet Laura's friends."

After the rest of the family had found their places at the table, they all joined hands. Pastor Greg asked Benard to say the blessing.

Warm with delight, he smiled. "I will do that, Pastor Greg."

After dinner, Greg released Ricky from his crate. The fair-sized black lab mix bounded to Pastor Benard and leapt up, placing both front paws on his chest. *Oops,* Greg thought. *I should have checked . . . I hope Pastor Benard likes dogs.*

Pastor Benard seemed even more startled when Ricky's wide pink tongue covered his face with sloppy kisses. Peels of laughter erupted around the room, and Greg rushed over to yank Ricky's collar.

"Come on, Ricky. That's enough love for now," said Greg.

Wiping his face with his hands, Pastor Benard stared in amazement at the beast allowed to live indoors. "You do not have animals outside on your property?" Benard tried to piece it all together. "I see, you let them run free in the house." He searched their faces to verify his observations, and took in their nods with one of his own. "I see."

Greg tried to shed some light. "Living in more of a city-type atmosphere, we can't let animals roam on our land. We would have a hard time confining them to our yard, and they would get run over."

Pastor Benard eyed Ricky warily. "In Kenya, dogs are for protection. I only let mine out at night after everyone is inside. He is not friendly like this one here." He pointed to Ricky, still unsure of him.

Greg smothered his grin. American ways must seem silly sometimes. "Pastor Benard," he said, "I'm going to show you where Americans keep their animals."

Benard's face lit up. "Thank you, Pastor Greg. I will look forward to seeing the animals."

"That is a big bird, Mama Sue. How did it fit in your oven?"

"Very carefully, Pastor Benard." Mama Sue set the golden brown turkey in the dining room. "The biggest challenge is finding a place to cook the rest of the meal." She motioned toward the table laden with bowls and platters of various colors, shapes, and sizes. Swarms of women continued bringing out rolls and butter, mashed potatoes and gravy, carrots and green bean casserole . . .

"There are so many choices! "How will I know what to eat?"

Carrying cranberry sauce and yams, Laura passed her mom in the doorway. "I'll explain, Pastor Benard. Don't worry. It will be like an adventure to taste everything!" She pinched his arm and hurried back to the kitchen.

Benard eyed a big fancy box of chocolates that a woman named Aunt Martha had brought. Light brown, dark brown. Round, rectangular, oval, square. Sprinkles, nuts, coconut. Complete with a bright red bow, the golden package appeared too beautiful to actually open and consume.

"Mama Sue," he asked, "are these candies really to eat or just to look at?"

Mama Sue smiled wide. "We're going to eat them after dinner, Pastor Benard. You'll get the first piece."

Relatives packed the house, and Benard could not remember all of the names. Such friendly people just like his family. Pangs of loneliness seeped into his heart, unbidden. He wished Pamela and the children could eat this feast with them today and wondered what they were doing right now. He checked the time. Pamela was probably getting the children ready for bed.

The doorbell rang, whisking him back into reality. He wiped away a tear and straightened. He must talk to his new friends now.

"Thanks for letting us mosey into your barn," Pastor Greg said to the dairy farmer on the outskirts of town. "Figured now was a good time with us already in here to pay for our tree."

"Don't mention it. Happy to help out."

Benard felt the farmer's eyes upon him as he carefully approached the milking area. *How in the world . . . the farmer used a metal machine to get milk from the animal?* Benard bent to examine one, trying to understand how it functioned. Tucking his hands in his pockets, he backed away. It looked like it would pain the animal.

After coughing loudly, the farmer explained. "We keep all of our cows in here, and we've got some chickens running around out back. They share a coop which is a small building where they lay their eggs."

Benard's eyes bulged as he surveyed the enormous building called the main barn. All of the cows kept in one place, together? He had never seen so many cows all at once. His glance flashed back to their host. He must be a very rich man. Benard extended his hand.

"Thank you for showing us your cattle."

The farmer returned the handshake and smiled. "The pleasure's mine, Pastor. It's not every day I get to talk to a native Kenyan."

"I still don't understand," Pastor Benard commented while shedding his hat and gloves on the car ride home. "Why did you kill this magnificent tree?"

Even though he had seemed to enjoy riding up the mountain in the wagon full of hay, Greg realized that Pastor Benard failed to grasp the connection between American Christmas tradition and destroying the life of a beautiful tree. He thought hard while he and David lugged the eight foot Douglas fir into the living room.

Pastor Benard stared as Sue, Laura, and Amy strung the branches with colored lights. Now he stood next to the tree, lightly rubbing his fingers over the branches as if to comfort them.

Great, Greg thought. *How am I going to explain this one?* He gulped and exchanged glances with Sue.

"Well, you see, the whole tree cutting and decorating is an American Christmas tradition that is centuries old."

Pastor Benard held up a hand. "You are telling me that every year you go out, kill a tree, bring it into your house, and put lights on it?"

The family of five nodded in unison.

"Why?"

Silence fell. Laura recovered first.

"I guess it must seem strange to you now that I think about it from your perspective." She giggled. "I guess we've just always done it. They're pretty to look at and fun to decorate with our family." She reached for a sparkly red ornament. "Would you like to help?"

Pastor Benard took it from her and guarded it as if he held the Hope Diamond.

"What do I do?"

Sue stepped in and pointed to a bare branch.

"Right here, Pastor Benard. Loop the hook over this branch."

Gingerly, he stooped and complied.

"Good job! That looks beautiful! Would you like to hang another ornament?"

Greg gazed at her with love. Leave it to Sue to make everyone feel great about themselves. His eyes panned the room. *My heart is so full, Lord! Thank You for blessing our home this Thanksgiving.*

Chapter Fifteen

Getaway

L ike this?" Mounds of fluffy yellow eggs emerged from the gooey raw substance that somehow disappeared with heat. This was not so bad. Benard continued stirring while his teachers looked on with approval.

"You're doing great, Pastor Benard."

He smiled at Laura. "You sound like Mama Sue."

Everyone giggled. Genevieve, Laura, and Lexi had insisted on helping Benard learn to make a few simple meals. They now stood in his tiny kitchen, peering over his shoulder.

"We call these scrambled eggs, Pastor Benard," said Genevieve.

Lexi leaned on the countertop behind her. "Yep. There are lots of ways to cook eggs. There's hard-boiled, over-easy, sunny-side up . . ." She stopped when his mouth fell open. "But scrambled will work just fine. Good job—looks like they're done."

"Thank you." He turned off the stove burner and retrieved four plates. "Please have eggs with me, ladies."

Everyone got a scoop of tasty scrambled eggs and a slice of toast. They prayed and then sat down to eat their manna from heaven together.

"Mmm, delicious. You're becoming a gourmet chef!"

Benard grinned. Laura had the gift of making every man feel like a king.

"Next lesson—spaghetti," Lexi said.

Benard was glad Lexi was there. He had gotten to know her through Laura and prayed for her daily.

"Wow, I have to go soon." Laura swallowed her last bite of toast. "Let's clean up quick!"

She rose and started gathering plates as the other girls wiped the table and cleared the stove. Picking up their backpacks and slinging them over their shoulders, they thanked Benard for the meal and hugged him tightly.

"Goodbye, my daughters. Thank you for the lesson!"

Laura and Lexi headed for campus after parting with Genevieve at the road.

"So Lexi, how are you doing? I mean, really doing?" For months, Laura had prayed for her friend and hoped she would one day let her see her ankles. Their friendship had blossomed, but Lexi still kept her ankles hidden.

"Okay." Lexi shrugged. "My ankles haven't improved. They've actually gotten pretty bad lately. Look, I have to drop something off at the admissions office. I'll see you later!"

Laura watched her go, feeling Lexi's pain as her own. *Let me help carry her burden, Lord.*

"Hello, Pamela. It is good to hear your voice. How are you and the children getting along?"

"We are doing fine, Benard. I planted some sugarcane last week." Pamela outlined her plan to sell dresses and various agricultural products using the land she now rented with Benard's library money. There would even be enough money to send Abraham and Betha to school!

"How are Jacob and Christine?"

Pamela sobered at the mention of her niece and nephew. Their father, Pamela's brother, had died a few weeks ago, and his wife could no longer take care of them.

"Doing poorly. They miss their father terribly, Benard." Pamela had taken them in temporarily until permanent arrangements could be made. Their options were few, and Pamela knew in her heart what she wanted to do if Benard was willing. "Could we adopt them, Benard?"

"Pamela, I was going to ask you the same question."

"Pastor Benard, guess what?" Laura bounded into his living room with the Sunday night crew and a white paper bag with a big yellow "M".

Bernard reached for the bag and smiled. She certainly was faithful about bringing chicken nuggets.

"A friend has offered to let our band use his trailer on Lake Murray for a retreat! Isn't that cool?" She whirled around the room while Chris and Teri laughed.

"We've all been so busy forming our new band, Tailor's Trail, with drummer Patrick Wheeling, it will be great to get away. Please say that you'll come!"

"Laura, I don't know. I have a lot of schoolwork—"

"I'll help you! And besides, we technically can't go without you. CIU policy."

"What policy?" Chris hopped in.

"One of CIU's rules is that all coed overnight activities must be chaperoned by an appropriate sponsor. It's simply to protect everyone's integrity."

Benard thought that it seemed to be a good rule and probably prevented a lot of trouble. "But I am a student also," he said. "How can I be a sponsor?"

Teri had an answer. "You are a happily married pastor, and you're over thirty. I think you'll pass."

Laura plopped down on the chair next to Benard's. "The best news of all is that Lexi said she would go with us!"

That was a miracle. Benard sat forward but resisted the urge to commit. "I do want to go." He paused. "I will pray about it, my friends. It sounds like a wonderful time."

SPRING BREAK 2003

"I'm so glad you came, Pastor Benard."

"Me too, Lexi." He had talked to her for quite a while as they relaxed on the back deck of the trailer. "Pamela would love it here. Why can't CIU let us commute from here. It is so peaceful and beautiful, like my homeland."

Lexi smiled. "South Carolina reminds me a little of Florida, where I grew up, but Florida is much warmer all year round than here. I really had to bundle up when I came to CIU."

The others joined them outside bringing tall, cool glasses of tea.

"I think we should have a time of prayer together," said Benard.

The others agreed. God had delivered them safely to this tropical paradise three days ago, and the group had spent their time singing, praying, studying, and having fun together. Benard would cherish these days forever.

Patrick, the drummer, shared a request, and they prayed over it together. They took turns sharing then praying. Lexi remained quiet. Benard sensed the reason.

"Lexi, my daughter, what is your trouble today?"

Lexi glanced at Laura and began to weep. Laura ran to her side and held her friend. Eventually, Lexi's tears subsided and she spilled the secret locked within her broken heart.

"For thirteen years, I have dealt with a scratching disorder called Lichen's disease. It's ugly, it's painful, and I hate having it." Her lip quivered, and tears streaked her reddened face. "I've done everything I know of to get rid of it . . . and I can't . . . my ankles . . ." Sobs consumed the suffering woman.

Everyone cried, and Benard moved to Lexi's chaise lounge. She stiffened, seeming to know what he would ask of her.

"Lexi, I want to pray for you. May I lay my hands on your ankles?"

"I've never shown anyone except my family . . ."

"Lexi," Benard said, "for years my mother has struggled with a similar condition. She scratches herself with twigs until she bleeds in order to get some relief. You are not alone, my daughter. We are your family in Christ, Lexi. We love you." Benard held out his hands.

Crying softly with her arm around Lexi, Laura remained silent.

Lexi's trembling hand inched down to her pant hem. Her breath came in short gasps between her sobs as she eased her clothing away and exposed the crimson scabs festering on her pale flesh. No one spoke. Weeping as one, they formed an unbreakable bond.

Benard carefully laid his palms over Lexi's wounds and asked God for her healing. When he finished, he removed his hands, and Laura reached down to place her hands on Lexi's ankles.

"O, Lexi, thank you! Thank you for letting us pray for you like this." They embraced and found themselves alone on the terrace.

"Wait, Lexi, stay right there!" Laura ran off and returned with a pail of water and a bar of soap.

Lexi shot her a puzzled look. "Laura, what are you doing?"

Laura took a seat on the slate floor and smiled. "Washing your ankles, my friend."

Chapter Sixteen

The Plan

MAY 2003

*B*enard beamed as he walked across the stage. He shook the hand of the dean and took the diploma signifying the completion of his Bachelor's degree. Only two more years, and he would have his Master's of Theology. It was really happening!

Once back in his seat, Benard lost himself in a flood of joyous tears. The Lord had been so good to him. In miraculous ways, money for his school bills had come in from churches, friends, and CIU. Anonymous private donors who had heard about his plight also wanted to help and had given generously. Benard now had no doubt the Lord had called him here and that He would see him through to the end.

Forgive me for not having enough faith, Lord.

"Congratulations, Pastor Benard!" Well-wishers surrounded him as the ceremony ended, and he turned to receive them.

SUMMER 2003

Summer break in his homeland with his beloved Pamela and children had gone all too quickly. What a joy it was to resume his duties overseeing the happenings at the orphanage and seminary. Even though Pastor Wilson had returned from Nairobi last semester to discipline the now-contrite seminary pastors, Benard knew he needed to speak with them himself to ensure that Pamela would be treated well. He also knew he needed to forgive them so that nothing would hinder the ongoing work of ministry. *God help me,* he prayed.

SEPTEMBER 2003

"Over here!" Laura flailed her arms above her head, and Chris and Genevieve motioned for Pastor Benard to join them at their table by a cafeteria window.

Happy to see them, he picked up his orange tray and made his way to them.

"Hi, Pastor Benard!" Laura bounded up and gave him a bear hug. "We were just talking about how excited we are for you. You're so close! You only have two years left to finish your Master's in Theology. Then, you can go back to your family and ministry!"

Her contagious exuberance dimmed for a moment. "I'll miss you so much, but I won't think about it right now," she said, pushing a pile of green beans around her plate. She sighed and looked out the window. "Kenya is where you belong. God made you for that place."

Pastor Benard nodded and spread his hands wide. "I believe that. My purpose is to help my people know Christ."

They smiled, a deep understanding passing between them.

Pushing his meal away, Benard rose and walked to the window. He looked far into the distance. "I must return to them."

That evening Benard paced his tiny bedroom. His mind raced. As he took a sip of water, he thought about how the orphanage had no running water. He sighed. His people needed so many things—things that he alone could not provide. But now, through his education, he had a deeper understanding of their needs and struggled to map out the best way to help them.

He hoped to bring some of his CIU friends to Kenya, knowing their presence would encourage the people greatly. All of the students had gifts and abilities that would prove invaluable in ministering to his community. He tried not to get too excited, but tonight he couldn't help it as he explored the possibilities running through his mind.

"You know, Lord," Benard prayed aloud. "You know everything about this. Please raise up Your workers and resources to help in a lasting way—a way that will preserve the spirit of my people."

"Your ministry is so multi-faceted, Pastor Benard," said Ben Byxbe. He could never tire of talking with Pastor Benard, a new friend he had met in class. "From the church plants to Friends of Christ to the seminary—wow! You are a busy guy."

"The Lord has blessed me with many faithful brothers and sisters," Benard said. "We work alongside each other as a team with Jesus Christ as our head."

Ever since they had met, Ben had found himself gravitating toward the effervescent Kenyan mover-and-shaker. Pastor Benard had a heart to change things about his culture, things that weren't quite right. What a vision caster! Yet, he was humble. Incredible.

"I took a ten-day survey trip to Agudo in South Nyanza over Christmas break with four others from Trinity Baptist Church," Ben said. "We fell in love with the Kenyan culture."

Pastor Benard cocked his head to one side. "That village is close to my home village, Wachara." He paused and studied Ben carefully. "Would you consider going back to Kenya? I would love for you to come and teach at AEST."

Ben's heart thudded loudly, and he hoped Pastor Benard could not hear it.

"Really? You want me to come to Ahero?" Ben ran his fingers through his hair and grinned. "Well, sure, I'll pray about it. I might be able to recruit a few more helpers to teach, serve with Friends of Christ, reach out to the street boys—whatever you need."

Pastor Benard flagged her down outside of the cafeteria. "Melissa! Hello, Melissa Hardy!"

She returned his wave. "Hi, Pastor Benard. Are you on your way to lunch?"

"Yes, I am."

"Me, too. I think some of our classmates will arrive shortly. We'll save a big table for everybody."

"Great!" He grinned. "Melissa, I want to thank you for helping me with that math problem after class today. I wrestled with it for many hours last night."

"You're welcome, Pastor Benard," she said with a smile. "Would you like help with math again this semester? I can tutor you," she offered.

He halted. "Would you? I had hoped I would be okay this year and not take up any more of your time, but I . . . that would be an answer to prayer."

Pastor Benard fell into step beside her. "Trying to keep numbers straight confuses me—and then I try to do it in English!" He shook his head. "It is very difficult for me."

"I'm sure it is. We'll start tomorrow."

FEBRUARY 2004

"My friends," said Benard to his chicken nugget group, "I invite all of you to Kenya this summer to help with the ministry there."

No one spoke as they sat in stunned silence.

"The Bible says that the harvest is plentiful but the workers are few. That is true." He shook his head sadly. "Friends of Christ needs volunteers who will visit orphans and widows in their distress. AEST seminary students desire deeper teaching about God and His Word. The streets of Kisumu and Ahero cry out for evangelists who will share the gospel with their people. With your beautiful songs and words of hope, you could win hearts for Christ and encourage the people."

He let the sentence hang and watched their faces. They seemed interested—good! With more patience than he felt, Benard waited for their response. He did not have to wait long.

Chris found his tongue first. "Kenya? Go to Kenya with you? To serve in the ministry—I like that!"

Genevieve looked at Laura, and both girls grew enormous grins.

"How long would we go for, Pastor Benard?" Laura asked.

"I am thinking ten weeks," he said. "I calculated that you would need a week to travel and get acclimated to your surroundings. Then, the next six weeks you would stay in Kisumu with families doing door-to-door evangelism. You would finish your time with Pamela and me in Ahero, teaching at the seminary."

Teri's eyes darted around the room. "There's enough time for us to raise support—maybe even our home churches would help us. I think it's a great idea! We all need to pray about it . . ."

Laura's eyes sparkled. "I'm planning to go home next weekend, and I'll talk to my parents about it. I would love to go."

Benard smiled. "I would love for you all to meet my family and serve beside me in the Lord's work. Thank you for considering doing this on your precious time off school."

"Mom, Dad, guess what?"

Here it comes, Greg thought. Laura had prepped them well, and he knew what was coming.

"Pastor Benard has invited Teri, Chris, Genevieve, and me to go to Kenya and serve in his ministry this summer!"

"Wow, that's exciting, honey," Greg said, sharing a look with Sue. Both parents smiled at their effervescent daughter, so full of life and love for this Kenyan pastor and his people. They had all come to think of Pastor Benard as family, and his offer appeared like the chance of a lifetime.

"Every Sunday night for years now, we've gone to his house and naturally become interested in his life." Laura paused dramatically. "And now, he wants us to share in it! Chris will teach New Testament, Genevieve will do music, and I'll do whatever. Pastor Benard mentioned traveling and speaking to different rural villages and tribes. I'll get more specific speaking topics closer to our departure date, but I simply want to go and help do whatever needs doing."

Her parents sat together on the sofa, holding hands and enjoying watching their daughter come alive with passion for a people she had never met but loved through the heart of one man. Beautiful.

Greg found his voice. "How can we say no?"

Laura squealed and ran to hug them. They all laughed together and savored the delight of the moment.

"There's no greater feeling as a parent than to have your child tell you that she wants to serve Jesus Christ. We're so proud of you, Laura, and of what God is doing in your life," Greg said around the lump in his throat. Sue could only nod as joyful tears rolled down her cheeks. Their daughter hugged them again.

"I really love you guys."

MAY 2004

"Twenty hours of curriculum?" Laura shook her head as she read the letter in her trembling hand. She planned to leave in one week! How was she going to pull this off?

"Mom, the dean of the college wants me to develop twenty hours of HIV/AIDS curriculum and teach it at AEST. Me!" She laughed hysterically, and her mother allowed herself a small giggle from the family room sofa.

"He's asking a twenty-year-old virgin to explain the intimate details of human sexuality and the need for abstinence!"

"You know, Laura, God will be the one getting the curriculum done, not you. What an incredible opportunity He has given you to train future leaders and teachers how to prevent the spread of a fatal disease and to protect the sanctity of sex in marriage!"

Laura pondered her mother's words.

"You're right, Mom. If this is how God wants to use me, He will figure it out." Laura leapt off her chair and headed upstairs. On her way up, she shot Mom a smile. "I'd better get busy!"

Chris got the call.

"Hi, Teri. You sound awful."

Teri dropped the bomb. "I'm not going to Kenya, Chris. The swelling in my lymph nodes has not improved."

Chris could hear the regret in Teri's voice. Maybe God was trying to tell them something. Maybe none of them should go. "I'm sorry to hear that, Teri. How are they treating it?"

"The doctor wants to do a biopsy . . . He says my immune system may not be up for exposure to diseases from halfway around the world . . . " Teri fell silent.

Poor guy. He had gone to so much trouble to line this thing up and get CIU to give them summer internship credits.

"Hey man, keep me posted on those results, will you? I think you're wise not to go if you're not feeling your best. The trip will prove tough enough for a healthy person, I'm guessing."

"You guys will be in my prayers," Teri said, sounding reassured. "Please take my support money with you—"

"Aw, Teri—"

"No really, I mean it. Some of my usual supporters actually told my mom that they didn't feel led to give this time. Now I know why."

Silence.

Chris broke it first. "Maybe we shouldn't go, Teri—"

"Pray about it, Chris," Teri encouraged. "Maybe God used me for communications on this end and will use you guys to serve over there. Don't get me wrong, it's killing me not to go . . . but God has his reasons for keeping me home." Teri gave a half-laugh. "Who knows? Maybe I would have loved it too much and never come back."

The two chuckled.

"I'm sure God has a plan in all of this, Teri."

"Take lots of pictures for me."

"You can count on it," Chris said.

Teri sighed loudly. "I'm going to tell the girls after class. I'll tell Pastor Benard . . . sometime. Please pray for me."

Chris gulped as tears filled his eyes.

"Will do." Chris hung up the phone and got down on his knees. "Lord, I'm willing to can this whole thing right now if You don't want us to go—just say the word. Whatever You want."

Part Four

Partnership

The body is a unit, though it is made up of many parts; and though all its parts are many, they form one body. . . . If one part suffers, every part suffers with it.

I Corinthians 12:12, 26

Chapter Seventeen

Americans in Kenya

SUMMER BREAK 2004

Mama, Mama, he's here! He's here!" All of the children scrambled outside as the matatu carrying their precious father lumbered toward the house.

Benard! Pamela gasped and then quickly smoothed her hair and skirt. She felt like a schoolgirl but didn't care. With eyes sparkling, she stepped outside as happy shouts erupted around her. Benard flew from the vehicle and scooped up as many children as he could hold, his eyes searching until he found hers.

He smiled, and her heart pounded.

Her Benard was home for the summer. She would enjoy every minute.

"It is good to see you and have you in my homeland." Benard clutched the back of his seat as the passenger van bounced down the uneven dung road. He chatted happily with his American friends. "I have many plans for you."

Laura, Chris, and Genevieve exchanged excited glances.

"Please tell us some of what we'll be doing," Genevieve said. "We know what you requested of us before we left the States was only a tentative outline."

Benard was glad they were excited. He wished he could take them all home with him to Ahero today, but the demands of the ministry would not allow them to come until their final three weeks in Kenya. That was okay. He was happy to share his friends.

"When you come later to Ahero, you will stay with Pamela and me, but in Kisumu, you will stay with members of the church family. Two widows and a pastor have each offered to take one of you into their homes. Each day, you will do door-to-door evangelism and help out at the local church.

"The leaders there are very discouraged." He felt the weight of their burden even as he explained it. "From little children on up to adults, the entire Sunday school program seems to be falling apart, and I thought the three of you could help . . ."

"Sure, Pastor Benard," said Laura. "We have years of Vacation Bible School, Summer Safari, Bible Study, and Youth Group under our belts. Maybe we can find some creative ways to come alongside the people and make suggestions as to how to keep their program fresh and new."

"We'll also be glad to help them with the musical end of things," Genevieve said.

Chris nodded his agreement. "Singing always adds another dimension . . ."

Benard grinned. This would be a wonderful summer.

Benard stood in the kitchen doorway, unsure how to broach his request. The Americans had done so much already. Chris had spent the last three weeks teaching New Testament at the seminary. Laura, too, had done lots of teaching, AIDS prevention brochure distribution, and visitation, while Genevieve had bustled about Ahero singing with her beautiful voice and teaching at AEST. Benard hated to ask, but he felt the opportunity was important.

"Does anyone want to go share with the union teachers at the boys' school?" Benard smiled at the three Americans seated around his dining room table.

"I'll do it," Laura volunteered. After teaching some lessons at the school over the previous three weeks, Laura had evidently become comfortable with the boys and the environment. Benard heaved a sigh of relief. "Thank you, Laura."

"Is it okay if I speak from Philippians?"

"Whatever you like, Laura. You will speak to a group of fifteen men who belong to a quarrelsome union." Benard shook his head. "They fight with each other all of the time." He checked his watch. "We'll leave first thing in the morning."

Laura smiled. "I'll be ready."

"What?" Laura stared at him with bulging eyes as if he had just asked her to walk five hundred miles barefoot.

Benard hesitated. "The headmaster of the school wishes for you to speak to the entire school."

Laura's face paled as she gulped. "How big is the school?"

"Besides the union teachers . . . between three and four hundred high school boys." Benard watched her closely. *Am I asking too much, Lord?* Peace washed over him, and he knew to encourage her.

"I can give you ten minutes to revise your talk. Laura, you must remember that God is the One who will make this happen."

She pondered his statement. "You're right, Daddy Benard. You're exactly right." With that settled, she grabbed a pen from her dusty backpack. "Ten minutes—got it!" She scurried off to a chair in the corner of the school office and flipped through her note cards with vigor.

Applause thundered through the gymnasium as Laura exited the stage. *Thank You, Lord,* Laura prayed as Pastor Benard gave her a thumbs-up. She grinned and waved him on-stage.

"Go get 'em." Her eyes sparkled.

A hush fell over the boys. *Now that's a miracle,* Laura thought. *Pastor Benard commands such a presence.* Her heart raced as he shared the gospel with the boys, talking about the death of Jesus and the reason for the cross. As Pastor Benard challenged the boys to examine their lives and make a decision for Christ, Laura prayed that many would come forward.

One by one, they came. Some shed tears, others smiled, but all one hundred and eighty who came forward that day accepted Christ and promised to live for Him.

Laura wept.

What was that? Somewhere in the dreamy world between consciousness and slumber, Chris thought he heard a strong voice rumbling through the house. *Again?* That had happened every morning since he had slept here. *What was it?* He roused a little more and realized that the noise indeed came from within Pastor Benard's house. Now totally awake, Chris held his head off the pillow and listened intently as the rumbling began again.

"O Lord, watch over Chris, Laura, and Genevieve. Please protect them during their stay here and give them health and stamina for the work You have brought them here to do. Use them, Lord. Use them to further Your kingdom here in Kenya."

Little tingles ran up and down Chris' spine. *Pastor Benard is praying for us? It is the crack of dawn!*

A muffled, feminine voice trickled through the quiet. "Thank You for healing Teri, Father, and we accept Your plan in not allowing him to come to Kenya this summer."

Mama Pamela too? Wow!

Always steady by her husband's side, Mama Pamela had proven herself to be as much a part of the ministry as Pastor Benard. She was an amazing picture of a true servant, overflowing with unselfish love for her family, her houseguests, and her church. Her tremendous faith to persevere through suffering had helped her children deal with the trial of going without.

They were quite a team. People who prayed—together. Conviction rose within Chris' spirit as he appreciated Pastor Benard and Mama Pamela in a new way. They put their faith into practice.

That's why God used them so powerfully.

Only a month after the trip taken by most of the Chicken Nugget Crew, Ben Byxbe from CIU and his team pressed their foreheads against the airplane windows after landing in Kisumu, Kenya. The tiny commuter plane had left some of them jittery, but their nerves had calmed as soon as they saw their friend.

"Welcome, everybody! Welcome to Kenya!" Pastor Benard smiled wide and opened his arms.

"Hi, Pastor Benard! We made it." Ben returned the pastor's embrace and then stepped aside so that his sister, Sarah Bothwell, could greet their friend.

"Hello, Sarah!" Pastor Benard embraced her warmly. "Hello, everybody!" Benard waved and bounced from person to person, herding the entire team out to a waiting passenger van. "We call this a matatu," he explained. "You must come and see Pamela. She has been busy preparing food all day for you."

Ben couldn't believe their trip was almost over. He zipped his suitcase shut and lifted it off the bed. Surprised, he raised the blue bag up to his waist and then set it down on the floor. Wow, his bag was much lighter. *Good,* he thought with a smile. He hoped his belongings would bless the people.

For the past nine weeks, Ben had served in various ways throughout Benard's vast ministerial organization. The men in his group from CIU had taught various subjects at the seminary while the women had primarily assisted with widow visitation, teaching the orphans, and checking in with guardians. Ben had enjoyed watching the students light up when Pastor Benard walked into their classroom, his humble yet commanding presence drawing each student close. You would have thought John Piper or Chuck Swindoll had just arrived.

Ben also remembered well his trip during the first week to Friends of Christ in rural Ahero. Small clusters of children had laughed and played together. The warm sun shone down on them as they joined hands, formed one large circle, and sang, "What a Mighty God We Serve." Their teacher stepped outside and smiled with approval, her face shining. She applauded and beckoned the children back inside.

Dozens of bright blue or pink-and-white uniforms flooded the crude one-room schoolhouse as the students found their places behind rickety wooden desks. The smell of cooking porridge filled the air, making tummies growl and heads turn. For many, the small bowl they received for lunch would be their only meal until tomorrow.

Ben noticed a jagged piece of chalkboard leaning against the front of the room and plastic-covered photographs of the children's parents lining the remaining walls. Every day, these colorful photos reminded the children of the powerful pain that bound their lives together.

Most of their parents had died from AIDS.

Pastor Benard saw Ben's pain. "Everybody in Kenya has been affected by death in their homes," he explained. "Therefore, when somebody in the community dies and leaves children behind, nobody cares."

"So the children continue to live with their remaining relatives?"

Pastor Benard nodded thinking how the endless cycle of death and mourning left everyone emotionally exhausted and forced the remaining relatives to cope with grieving orphans.

"Yes," he said, "but the families find it easier to cope with the kids living in their homes when Friends of Christ takes the children five days per week for school. We give every child lunch, education, and spiritual nourishment. Their relatives see the benefit and usually support our efforts."

The two men left the school in silence as Ben, overwhelmed with compassion for the children, pondered the experience. He had never known an orphan before, and he had just looked into the faces of forty-eight.

Thank You, Lord, for what You're doing here. It's truly amazing.

Friends of Christ Orphanage - Ahero

Laura Wollenhaupt

Chris Matthews, Laura, Lexi McNair, Patrick Wheeling

Laura & Sue Wollenhaupt

Chapter Eighteen

Laura

AUGUST 14, 2004

As the clock hands approached midnight, an exhausted Benard stood in the terminal smiling as Ben Byxbe approached.

"Welcome back to school, Pastor Benard. Ready for your final year?"

"Yes, I am! Hello, my friend. It is good to see you."

Even though Ben had mustered up a smile and a warm hug for the incoming Kenyan, Benard immediately sensed that Ben's heart was heavy. "Is anything wrong, Ben?"

His eyes welled with tears. "I don't know how to tell you this, Pastor Benard."

Ben paused for what seemed like an eternity. Benard braced himself. Something was very wrong.

"There's been a terrible accident . . ." Ben's voice broke as he scanned the nearby area. "Come. Let's go sit on that bench."

He grabbed Benard's arm and guided him through the maze of luggage and bystanders. With every step they took, Benard's uneasiness grew. He slipped off his lightweight jacket that had now become heavy and hot.

Ben resumed his story. "I need to tell you what happened, Pastor Benard . . . Yesterday, the Wollenhaupt family headed down to Disney

World in three separate cars. Laura had just gotten her driver's license, so she drove her car down with Amy. They followed David, Sue, and Greg while Lexi and their friend, Danny, drove behind Laura and Amy's car. They opted to caravan because school starts this week, and they planned to drop the kids back at CIU on the way home . . ." Ben's voice trailed off.

After a minute, he coughed and resumed his account of August 14, 2004.

"It was a bright, sunny day, and Laura appeared to handle driving well until right inside Virginia where she . . . she lost control of her vehicle somehow and crossed the median. An eighteen-wheeler hit her car head-on at full speed . . . The impact tore the car into four pieces. Later, the state policeman couldn't recognize the make and model."

Benard felt numb all over. He could not believe he was hearing this. *Sweet Laura* . . . He wiped his eyes.

"Sue and Greg didn't actually see the accident but soon noticed the girls weren't behind them anymore. By the time they turned around and headed back to the scene, Lexi and Danny had pulled over and started helping. An EMT and a nurse had also stopped to assist. Sue ran to Laura and sang to her, stroking her arm until the ambulance arrived. Greg ran to Amy . . .

"When they got to the hospital, the staff had already rushed Laura into surgery, but . . . She didn't make it, Pastor Benard. Her aorta suddenly burst after three hours of surgery." Ben stopped and blew his nose. "They almost lost two daughters that day. It's a miracle Amy survived."

Sorrow flooded Benard. He wept as he and Ben embraced. *O Father, help us now.* Giant tears streamed down his face as he mourned the loss of his beloved friend.

The last time he was in this church, Laura was here. Benard scanned the olive green padded pews, large stage, and musical instruments scattered about. How he wished she could worship with them today! He rubbed his sweaty palms down his tan pants and fingered the top button of his khaki shirt. *Lord, give me the strength to say what I must.*

"Hi, Pastor Benard."

Genevieve, Teri, and Chris stood near his shoulder. Benard rose and greeted them.

"Come, sit with us," Teri said. Even though Teri's health issues had resolved, he looked terrible under the intense burden of grief.

Benard gratefully followed them into a pew and sank into its soft cushion. After a few minutes, Lexi and Danny joined them. There was so much sadness in these young people. Such sadness.

Benard eyed the packed sanctuary. *Laura, my friend, you should see how your people love you.*

A hush fell over the room as Pastor Greg and Mama Sue walked up the aisle. Many had offered their condolences to the family in the gym prior to the service, and the couple already appeared exhausted. David followed them in, pushing Amy's wheelchair. Once the Wollenhaupts had settled in their seats, the big gray coffin was placed at the front.

Sweet Mama Sue and Papa Greg! Tears rolled down Benard's cheeks, and he did not try to wipe them away. *Sweet Amy. David.*

A door opened, and Laura's pastor walked onto the platform. He welcomed everyone and stated that many would take part in the morning's service.

Speaker after speaker shared what Laura had meant to them over the years, and the band played some of her favorite songs. Dr. Steve Baarendse, one of Laura's professors, took part, extending greetings from Dr. George Murray, the President of CIU.

"Laura lived more in her twenty years than most people do in eighty." The professor sniffled and moved on with a smile. "She did not waste her life or make a promise she couldn't come through on. She was faithful in the little things and uncommonly deep in her thinking. Laura loved the Lord with her mind despite living in a shallow generation, and she was uncommonly concerned about the unsaved . . ."

Benard listened as more friends and family shared, his stomach churning when his turn arrived. All eyes fell upon him as he made his way down the aisle. After laying a wad of tissues on the lectern, he gripped it with both hands.

"I am Pastor Benard Ondiek, friend of Laura. I met Laura on a Thursday after Western Civ. class. She walked right up to me and asked me my name. 'This class is very difficult,' she said. 'Do you understand what Dr. Layman is saying?'

"I said, 'It is very hard.' She said, 'Pastor Benard, I am going to help you.' Then she would ask me how I did on my work. 'I passed it,' I would say. She would jump up and down and say, 'You are working so hard! What did you get?' 'I got a B+,' I would answer. 'You've worked so hard, Pastor Benard,' she would praise me. 'You are so good.'

"Our relationship continued like that. I have two sons and three daughters, very close friends to me at CIU. Losing one of them is very difficult as an international student, you know.

"She was a faithful lady, and she would never lie. 'I will find a chance to help you, Pastor Benard,' she would say, not only to me but also to other international students. Laura made herself available anytime. Even if she was busy, she would sit down and talk to me or listen to me.

"Laura was always doing what the Lord wanted her to do. She was teachable and wanted to learn. She was very brilliant and knew many things. She asked me so many things about Kenya . . ."

Benard launched into details of her trip to his homeland and how she shared his vision for the church in Africa.

"Laura was a dynamic lady. She motivated the entire class in Kenya, teaching them how to handle their suffering and how to help those suffering around them. She went to a high school that has had a bad reputation for years and years, so bad in fact that they go on strike quite often. I shared the gospel with them, and Laura spoke from Philippians. One hundred and eighty boys accepted Christ that day. When I went back to follow up, the headmaster thanked me. He said, "The key leaders of the strikes in the school have accepted Christ, and now we have peace.'

"Laura was a great, great lady." Benard opened his worn Bible and read Psalm 84. "I'm going to miss her a lot.

"I told her never to compromise the principles of Christian living for worldly nonsense. Laura said, 'Pastor Benard, I will not compromise.' She surely lived the whole of her life loving the Lord. One day she will ask us, 'What did you do after I rested?' I want to sing a song I taught to Laura that teaches us all to 'Let the Lord Have His Ways.'"

Lord, help me do this for Laura.

Benard opened his mouth, and song flowed through his lips. No one stirred as the acappella melody rang through the church. Benard finished the song, picked up his tissues, and walked across the stage. After he hugged Lexi on the stairs, she took her place in front and smiled.

"Laura always said, 'I can't believe I know someone as famous as Pastor Benard.'"

The audience laughed, and Benard sunk into his seat. *Me? Famous?* He surveyed the crowd. *I think you were quite famous, Laura.*

Lexi began to share about her Lichen's Disease and how Laura had prayed for her. Benard smiled. What a miracle it was for Lexi to talk openly about her deepest secret.

"One day, Laura asked to see my ankles. She knew it would be hard, but she wanted to be a part of it. 'Lexi,' she said, 'it hurts me so much that you have to deal with this kind of pain, and it hurts Jesus even more . . . I want to help you.'" Tears flowed down Lexi's cheeks.

"Every night at school, Laura came to my room with a bucket, brush, and soap. She would say, 'I want to serve you the way Jesus would serve you.' It didn't matter how tired she was. She came every single night. She didn't wash my ankles for recovery; she did it because she loved me. The root of our relationship was Jesus Christ . . .

"In order to know Laura the most, you have to know Christ."

Lexi walked off the stage. After a few more people shared, Laura's pastor, Howard Lawler, reclaimed the podium.

"I was stunned when I got the news. Laura epitomized life, and the natural question that comes to mind is, 'Why so young?' Maybe it's because she has already made the rest of us look bad enough."

Soft chuckling rippled among the audience.

"I know when I'm in the presence of my betters . . ." Pastor Howard paused.

"Psalm 90 says, 'Teach us to number our days.' Laura lived out every one of hers, the ones that, according to Psalm 139, God had planned long before her life began. Don't undercut the confidence she had . . . it's like taking the very heart out of the person who so touched you.

"Laura jam-packed her days with lasting value and spiritual depth. She didn't have to rack up years in order to make her mark here on earth. She was a good person because she was on her way to heaven, not because she did good things." Through his tears, he smiled.

"I can hear her saying, 'You make sure you make that clear.'"

Laura Beth Wollenhaupt
October 22, 1983 – August 14, 2004

Chapter Nineteen

Moving Mountains

FALL 2004

*T*here he is, Alicia," Melissa said, waving across the cafeteria at Pastor Benard. His face lit up, and he motioned the two sisters over to his table. "I'm so glad you get to meet him."

Alicia had hoped for such an opportunity during her first year at CIU because Pastor Benard would graduate in the spring. Holding her orange plastic tray laden with pasta primavera, Alicia smiled and said nothing. So this was the pastor Melissa had not only tutored in math but also raved about for the past three years. He must be quite a man. Alicia filled her milk glass and then followed Melissa to the table.

"Melissa!" Pastor Benard stood and embraced her. He then eyed Alicia. "Is this your younger sister that I've heard so much about?"

Melissa nodded proudly. "In the flesh. Alicia Hardy, Pastor Benard Ondiek."

Alicia held out her hand. "It's a pleasure to meet you. Melissa's wild about Kenya thanks to you, Pastor Benard."

More students paused to greet him on their way to the exit. Making a point to greet each person individually, Pastor Benard glowed as he spoke with a dozen passersby. He smiled easily and seemed to know everyone in the cafeteria. He finally rejoined Melissa and Alicia at the table with a few more students.

"I'm sorry, ladies. I had to say hello."

"That's okay, Pastor Benard," Melissa said. She gestured to the new arrivals with a forkful of buttered carrots. "Who are your friends?"

For the next thirty minutes, the entire group engaged in a fun, get-to-know-you type of conversation. After most of the circle completed the typical "Where are you from?" and "What's your major?" questions, Pastor Benard spoke of his homeland, his ministry, and his family.

Alicia sat, intrigued. What an interesting life he led. She noticed the surety in his eyes and his countenance that radiated such joy. Incredible in light of the story he just told about almost being sent home because he couldn't pay his tuition bill last month. She found herself drawn to this man, so full of vigor and passion for the things of God and for serving His people.

Moved by his sense of urgency and obligation, Alicia rubbed her clammy palms down the thighs of her blue jeans as conviction stung her. He had given so much and seemed driven to obey God—no matter what. Pastor Benard's booming voice broke into her thoughts.

"Who among us wants to go to Kenya?"

He looked right at her. His question hung in the air, looming over Alicia like a storm cloud pursuing parched countryside. That would be so cool. She wondered if Melissa was considering it. Alicia studied her sister and took a bite of a whole wheat roll. That would make perfect sense. Alicia took another bite. Maybe she could go with Melissa . . . It wouldn't hurt to ask . . .

"Just out of curiosity, Pastor Benard, when would you go?"

"Next summer."

"I'm so glad you're here with me, Pamela." Beaming, Benard drank in the sight of her standing in the airport terminal. How had he ever done this with her halfway around the world? She smiled, and his heart raced. She had come to the Untied States for Easter and would stay through his graduation in May. Then they would fly home together. To stay.

Benard pressed the doorbell of the Wollenhaupt home, elated at the opportunity to bring his bride to the home of his dear friends. Pamela smoothed her hair and gave him a half-smile.

"They will love you, Pamela."

Pastor Greg swung the door open wide. "Pastor Benard, Mama Pamela! Welcome!" He embraced them both.

Mama Sue followed right behind him. "Please come in."

As they settled into the family room, the doorbell rang again. Grabbing her purse off the end table, Mama Sue popped up. "Sounds like dinner's here."

Pamela's jaw dropped. "Dinner brought right to the house—in a box? Everything is so easy." She stared as Mama Sue handed the Pizza Hut delivery boy a twenty dollar bill in exchange for the hot, aromatic boxes. "How does he keep it hot?"

Mama Sue giggled as she led the way to the kitchen with the scent of pepperoni wafting behind her. "The delivery boy carries a special bag with him that wraps the pizza in a material equivalent to a thousand potholders."

Pamela's eyes widened when Mama Sue lifted the lid and revealed a perfect circle of crust, cheese, and pepperoni. "Dinner is served!"

After saying grace, they all took slices of the savory pie, and after showing Pamela how to eat it, Pastor Greg and Mama Sue sobered.

"We still want to come to Kenya, Pastor Benard," Pastor Greg said.

Benard looked with compassion upon the grieving couple and exchanged a glance with Pamela.

"We believe the Lord will use this trip to bring healing from Laura's death."

"I believe that as well, my friends," Benard said. "But please, however the Lord is leading you, know that I will understand." Even though the trip had been planned for months, Benard would cancel the whole thing with just one word from his beloved friends. Anything to ease their pain.

"So, when should we buy the tickets?" Mama Sue allowed herself a smile as she posed the question.

They all laughed together and continued talking through plans until late in the night.

"We've never had a medical team come to Kenya." Pamela spoke with quiet awe. "Most of the people have never seen a doctor."

Pastor Greg snapped his fingers. "Hey, that reminds me, do you two know about the medical students from Kenya that rotated through Dr. Scott Rice's pediatrics practice a few months ago?"

The couple shook their heads.

Pastor Greg continued his story.

"Well, it turns out that as the medical team leader for our trip, Dr. Scott asked them to come and help us when we set up the field hospital in Wachara. A total of up to five medical students might come."

Pamela gasped and Benard grinned.

"That means more people will get treatment," Benard said. "Praise the Lord! He has provided once again."

"Congratulations, Benard." Pamela had finally gotten him alone after the beautiful graduation ceremony. "I am so proud of you."

She thought over the past four years. All of the fear, the hunger, the constant worry and pressure to protect and provide. And poor Benard. Coming to a new country with little money, no job, broken English. God had proven faithful, and they were thankful. Both of them had grown through this difficult time apart, and they loved each other more because of it.

"Thank you, Pamela." He smiled. "I could never have done this without you. You have been a rock through all of this, and I want to thank you for supporting me." Tears ran down his cheeks. "I know you sacrificed a lot."

"So did you. We are in this together, my Dearest Friend."

"I knew you would come back, Ben." Only days after graduation, Benard welcomed his seven CIU friends with a happy heart. "Genevieve, my daughter." He embraced her, then Alicia. "Are you ready to work with the street boys, Alicia?"

Her exuberance shone. "I'll serve wherever you need me to, Pastor Benard. I came to help you and am excited to do so."

He welcomed the others and led them to their host families.

Most of the team spent their time teaching and preparing lessons for either Friends of Christ or AEST, while Alicia found herself with Ben Byxbe and Pastor Benard visiting the street children of Kisumu.

"I want you both to meet Pastor Chris." Pastor Benard embraced the young pastor warmly. "Pastor Chris helped me plant many churches and now spends a lot of time trying to keep the street boys from seeking help from the Harney Krishna group across the street."

Pastor Chris nodded. "They meet the boys' physical needs but not their spiritual needs."

As Pastor Chris shared how Pastor Benard had discipled him and asked him to partner in the ministry, Alicia perceived him to be a quiet yet genuine man with a huge heart. How blessed the boys were to have two men care so much about them. She felt honored to serve with them.

"I have other ministries, but this is the one that makes me most happy," Pastor Benard said.

"The attitudes of the street boys are gradually changing due to the impact Pastor Benard has had on them," Pastor Chris said. "He speaks with them like a father and they listen."

Pastor Benard threw an arm around Pastor Chris' shoulders. He waved toward Alicia. "We are a team, doing God's work, with His help, for His glory."

"Does anyone know the story of Joseph?"

Alicia's translator rattled off the question in Luo as a dozen pairs of big brown eyes stared back at her.

"His ten brothers threw him in a pit because they were jealous of him. Their father favored Joseph over all the other sons." She paused again. They seemed to be listening. "Instead of leaving Joseph in the pit to die, the brothers sold him as a slave to traveling businessmen from Egypt."

Fury filled some of the boys' eyes. Others appeared amazed. One boy spat a comment, and Alicia waited for the translator to finish so that she could continue.

"But he was their brother, their own flesh and blood!" the translator said.

She prayed for wisdom, knowing that Scripture often brought hidden hurts to the surface.

"Betrayal, especially by those we love most, hurts. Deeply. Have any of you felt this kind of pain in your families?"

Many nodded, and the boys began talking all at once. The translator struggled to keep pace with them, and as Alicia listened to their terrible stories, she praised God for making a way into the hurting hearts seated at her feet.

"Our goal," said Pastor Benard, "is to show the boys affection in a godly way. For many tender years, they have lacked familial love, but when the boys feel loved by us, they open up because they feel like one of us. Only then can we help them. Most of them have tremendous emotional and physical needs due to their glue addictions."

"Glue?" Alicia shot Ben a puzzled glance.

Pastor Chris hopped in. "Sniffing glue, also known as huffing, makes them high. They feel stronger and better able to cope with their problems. It's cheap, easily acquired, and serves to suppress their appetites and make them feel warm at night." His eyes watered. "They don't understand how bad it is for them."

Nodding, Pastor Benard continued. "Some of the boys, like Elvis, have not yet turned to glue. They come to the street, realize it holds no hope for them, and fight living their lives as street boys. Elvis wants to go to school . . ." Pastor Benard's voice broke.

"Elvis is a good boy and speaks English well. He has never asked me for food or clothes—just school. He is bright and knows that education will keep him from a life on the street. If he can save enough money to go all of the way back home, he will go, but usually the boys get too hungry to save for bus fare. Sometimes, they turn to older street boys for help and become puppets in their hands."

"Sort of like pimping?" Alicia asked.

"Yes." Pastor Benard nodded. "Not of a sexual nature, but a financial one. The older boys provide protection while the younger ones steal and beg. The older boys take their share of the profit by force, realizing that people will not give as generously to older boys." He gazed into the distance. "It is a vicious cycle."

Pastor Chris clasped his mentor's arm, eyes sparkling with encouragement.

"We must do what we can as God gives us opportunity."

Pastor Chris and family.

Pastoral team that supports Benard's ministry.

Chapter Twenty

Team of Faith

LATER THAT SUMMER

Finally arriving in front of Pastor Benard's house, Greg dragged himself out of the crowded matatu. The team had been forced to separate in Nairobi due to a mix-up with the plane tickets. As team leader, Greg had stayed behind to accompany five ticketless women to Benard's house once the airline resolved the issue. Greg's spirit lifted as he opened the door and greeted the rest of the team. It was great to have everyone back together again.

"Hey, everybody!" Pastor Benard and Mama Pamela beamed.

Along with several women from the church Mama Pamela had made savory dishes and filled the table with grilled tilapia, lentils, ugali, bananas, and beverages. As they ate and relaxed in the Ondiek's living room, the travelers began strategizing for the coming weeks of ministry.

Greg outlined the plan. "Amy and Angie will help with the orphans at Friends of Christ while Lo and I teach at the seminary this week. Tomorrow, the rest of you will head to Wachara with Pastor Benard to run the medical clinic." Greg rubbed his hands together and panned the group. "Who has questions?"

The group remained silent but excited.

Pastor Benard cleared his throat. "Pastor Greg, would you preach at chapel for one hour every day this week in addition to teaching the classes we talked about?" Pastor Benard gave him a most irresistible smile. "I know the students would love hearing from you."

Whew! Greg smiled, thankful he had packed his old sermon notes. "I can do that," he said.

"The people would like to meet you tonight," Pastor Benard continued. "We will go to the church."

Greg almost dropped his water bottle. "Tonight?" He struggled but then realized he needed to maintain a gracious attitude for the sake of his host. "If you think we should—"

"Pastor Greg, it is very important for all of the people to welcome your team tonight. They will feel included in your ministry that way. Most of you will leave in the morning and . . ."

As Pastor Benard spoke, Greg picked up on his friend's sudden stiffness and pleading eyes. The guy had gone through so much to line this up for them. He observed Mama Pamela gathering dishes from the table, keeping her eyes lowered. Greg swallowed, trying to ignore the heaviness threatening to press his eyelids shut. This meeting was important to Pastor Benard.

"We understand, Pastor Benard," said Greg. "It's not a problem, right gang?"

The group followed his lead, murmured their agreement, and rose to slip their shoes on.

Pastor Benard smiled and sighed loudly. "Thank you. Thank you for doing this when you are all so tired. We will get you to bed soon."

What beautiful singing! Sue glanced around with a smile at the colorfully adorned women lifting their voices and clapping their hands. The music stirred her soul, and she found herself wishing she could speak Luo.

After the fifty congregants sat down, Pastor Benard introduced the team. "First I would like to introduce Papa Laura and Mama Laura."

Sue gasped, feeling the red hot pain pierce through her. Tears welled as the people moaned and nodded at the mention of the vibrant young lady they had come to deeply love. Everyone cried.

"Laura came to Kenya to help our people. She succeeded in many ways, and we called her our friend. Even though she will not return to us, God has raised up sixteen Lauras and brought them to Kenya." Pastor Benard wiped his eyes. "We thank God for this."

"We're almost there." Benard had searched for weeks to secure a place for them to work, and everyone's excitement grew as the vans approached the site. Nothing could have prepared the team members for what lay ahead. The dung road lined with green trees and bushes suddenly became hard-packed earth lined with tall golden grass, parting into a magnificent, wide-open field. Along the far side, tribesmen had fashioned a makeshift hospital out of bamboo poles, plastic and canvas tarps, and white bed sheets.

With welcoming hands extended, many people came to greet the Americans, and the air filled with murmurs. Curious children giggled as they shyly touched team members and then ran away. One of the villagers told them that earlier in the day "the field was full of people waiting to see you."

The team gulped, humbled. Their hands and arms unpacked supplies, but their minds asked the question, *How can we help so many?*

So this was where Pastor Benard had grown up. Sue surveyed the modest parcel of land and its simple dwelling. Some chickens and goats wandered freely within the confines of the property bordered by a wood and wire fence. In the far corner, the infamous squatty sat at the end of a well-worn path, and the workshop lay adjacent to the house.

"Mama Sue, I want you to meet my parents," Pastor Benard said.

"I'd be honored, Pastor Benard."

He helped her up the steps and into the Ondiek living room where his mother sat in a low-to-the-ground chair.

"Mama," he said in a gentle tone. "Mama Sue is here."

His mother's face lit up, and she craned her neck to see Sue returning her smile.

"It is good to meet you, Mama," Sue said with great warmth as she took the older woman's hands in hers. "Thank you for opening your home to us."

The matriarch nodded, pleased. The two women chatted with Pastor Benard while the other team members made their way into the room for the evening meal. They had gone to so much trouble for the team. Multiple women brought out dish after dish of native food. Sue had a lot to learn from their hospitality. Apparently, some families had moved out of their homes for the week in order to accommodate the team. Americans without extra beds typically offered the sofa. What a beautiful, selfless gesture.

With a grateful heart, Sue bowed her head as Pastor Benard said grace.

Early the next morning, the clinic tarp opened to the rapidly forming line of patients. People came from all around. Some traveled in wheelbarrows, some on bicycles, and others on foot, having walked over twenty-five miles. One man lay near the tent's entrance on a stretcher carried by five of his closest friends.

The families talked easily with the team about their health concerns. Some did not have any present ailments but just wanted to see a doctor. Benard took it all in as he stood in a corner of the tent, his eyes wide and filled with joyful tears. Perhaps someday they would have a permanent hospital in this village, but for now, he would simply be thankful and remember this day.

Many patients filtered through the makeshift hospital. Old and young. Male and female. Rich and poor. Illness did not discriminate. As Benard meandered down the aisle, he peered into an exam room and overheard Dr. Scott diagnosing a small boy with a bulging stomach.

"You have a nasty case of worms, Son. What have you been eating?"

The boy looked the doctor square in the eye. "Dirt."

Dr. Scott froze. "Dirt?"

The child nodded.

"Why?"

"I was hungry."

Benard wept.

He moved onto the next partition, his heart heavy. One of the women from the team held a crying baby. Stained, soiled clothing hung on the child like rags. The infant's pencil-thin arms flailed about as tears of frustration and hunger poured down her sallow cheeks. A boy, maybe six years old, proudly bundled the baby after the exam and hoisted her onto his back. With tears in her eyes, the woman bent down and placed a hand on his shoulder. "You're doing a good job."

The boy glowed and walked out into the crowd.

Only then did the woman notice Pastor Benard watching the scene. "Their mother died the night we arrived in Wachara."

He nodded. He had already spoken to the husband.

Benard studied the woman from the team as she circled the tent, rummaging through boxes and bags. She stopped and stood before him, wringing her hands.

"Pastor Benard, the baby was hungry, and I couldn't feed her," said the woman. She scanned the clinic again, but her anguished eyes quickly returned to Benard. "I have no food for her. If only I had the formula from my office . . ." She wept openly.

"I can't feed her, Pastor Benard. I can't feed her!"

Benard threw back the tent flap and disappeared into the field. He had seen enough. The woman with HIV who feared telling her husband. The older man needing inserts for his shoes but not finding any. The little boy who needed glasses. The starving baby girl . . .

He must find a quiet place to pray. Finally, far away, Benard knelt in the grass and raised his hands to the sky.

"Father in heaven, I beg You to help Your people. Bring them the care they need. Grant us opportunities to tell them about You, the Great Physician and Healer. O Lord, have mercy on Your people who suffer greatly."

The Americans had brought a ministry team as well as a medical team to Wachara. One young man named Josh told the people about the love of Jesus Christ. Benard searched their faces, encouraged. They were listening to him.

"If anyone would like to know more about how to have a personal relationship with God through His Son, Jesus Christ, please join me over by the bicycles. I'd love to talk with you." Josh turned and headed for the edge of the crowd. Suddenly, an entire mass of people rose and followed him, curious to know more about this Jesus.

Benard stood with his mouth open. *Thank You, Lord. After all these years of hardened hearts . . . thank You for what You're doing in this place.*

Back in Ahero for the second leg of the trip, Benard briefed the American speakers about their audience and introduced them to their translators. Benard paced the church aisle as he spoke, excitement coursing through his veins. This was going to be great!

"We expect over fifteen hundred women will attend the conference. The church will fill up by the end of the week because many will still be traveling during the first two days of the talks. Also, the seminary students will attend the conference in order to help lead discussion groups for Pastor Greg and Mama Sue. We want to give them a chance to practice the counseling skills they learned from Pastor Greg last week. Any other tasks you can give them to do while the conference is in session will be fine. They are here to assist you."

The speakers expressed their gratitude for the help and proceeded to find a seat for the opening talk given by Mama Sue.

Pastor Greg sauntered up. "Pastor Benard, where's Dr. Scott?"

"Dr. Scott, Don, and Danni went to the orphanage to give all of the kids a medical exam. They should be back this afternoon."

Greg smiled. "That's fantastic!"

Don, one of the team members, watched Mama Pamela and the kids scrub the floor and the many pairs of dung-coated shoes on the front porch. Always serving. He continued reading his Bible while Pastor Greg dozed on the sofa and Dr. Scott prepared his notes for tomorrow morning's sermon.

Pastor Benard bustled into the room, saw Don, and lit up. "Hello, Don."

Uh oh, Don thought. *It looks like he's got something for me to do . . . Maybe he was serious about me preaching tomorrow!*

"Don, you will preach at Bondee tomorrow."

Pastor Greg popped one eye open.

Don gulped and attempted to compose himself. He would only have a few hours to prepare an hour-long sermon. "When were you going to tell me?"

Pastor Benard looked shocked and came right back. "I told you yesterday."

Pastor Greg grinned but said nothing.

Don smiled good-naturedly. "I guess you weren't kidding then."

"No, I never kid, Pastor Don." Pastor Benard giggled.

Dr. Scott glanced up from his mountain of papers. "Pastor Benard, if Pastor Greg is preaching in Kisumu, I'm preaching in Ahero, and Don is preaching in Bondee, where are you preaching tomorrow?"

All of Pastor Benard's teeth shone. "I love it when my American friends come to visit me."

"This is the land I believe God has given my people."

Pastor Greg and Dr. Scott followed Benard to a grassy plot contained within a wood and wire fence.

"This is beautiful, Pastor Benard," said Dr. Scott. "Where exactly are we?"

"About six miles outside of Wachara." Benard waved his hand

toward the five acre expanse. Pleasure permeated his voice and radiated from his body. "I pray that in twenty years, God still gives me life. I want to see the vision He has given me come to pass ... to see a hospital, an orphanage, foster homes, and a church built for my people.

"We're standing on the land for the orphanage. We must pay $10,000 more before the deadline. I don't know how God will provide this money."

Pastor Benard patted a fence post and fought to maintain control. "I put up this fence to claim it as ours. But now, if I must take it down, it will tell the people that God could not do this, and it will be a great discouragement." He swallowed hard and closed his eyes. Opening them, he continued.

"God has not failed us thus far. He is using this to increase our faith in Him to move this Mount Kilimanjaro. My people struggle so much ... the obstacles, the warfare are endless because He is working mightily among us."

He looked into the eyes of his two friends. "I believe He will accomplish this. And much more."

The temporary medical clinic in Wachara.

A little girl steps onto a scale for the first time.

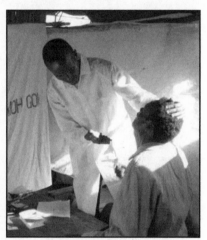

A medical student, Stephen, treats a patient.

People came from surrounding areas and lined up for treatment.

A family that had walked to the clinic.

Sue ministering to the crowd.

A table used by the clinic.

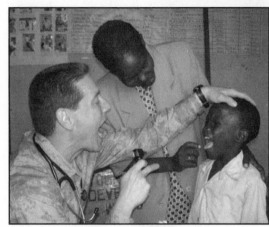

Dr. Scott Rice examines an orphan.

Pastor Albert translates for Abram, a medical student who took time off school to help at the clinic right before exams.

Wachara women cook for the American medical team.

The table spread with food inside the Ondiek family homestead.

Sue and the leaders of the 2005 Women's Conference at the Ahero Church

Pastor Greg
Wollenpaupt
teaching
counseling
skills to the
women.

Mama Pamela
greets
the students.

Pastor Greg taught counseling skills to AEST students
the week prior to the conference.

The 2005 Women's Conference at the Ahero Church.

Rizpah Ondiek,
Pastor Benard's mother.

Nurse Donna Frank cares for young mothers and children
in a makeshift clinic at the conference.

Part Five

Perseverance

Consider it pure joy, my brothers,
whenever you face trials of many kinds,
because you know that
the testing of your faith develops perseverance.

James 1:2-3

Chapter Twenty-one

The Accident

SEPTEMBER 2005

*B*enard wove his way through the crowded streets of the Ahero market in his white two-door car. Two of his daughters, six-year-old Dorothy and eight-year-old Melissa, rode with him in silence, staring at the mass of people, cars, and bicycles clogging the narrow streets. He could not wait to get home. He had awakened before dawn to pray with a new widow, and now, aching with fatigue, he wondered what Pamela had made for dinner.

The warm September day made his eyelids heavy, and he allowed his thoughts to wander as the vehicle picked up speed on the outskirts of the city. Summer would soon be here. He glanced at the girls in his rearview mirror. Dorothy had succumbed to the drone of the engine and leaned against her sister's cozy shoulder, but Melissa fought her drooping lids by waving her fingers one-by-one out the window.

Benard hid his smile. *O Lord, how I love my girls! I thank You for them . . .*

The sound of crashing metal pierced the air. By the time Benard returned to the present, his car rolled off the road, spiraled over the bank, and flipped five times. Benard's heart quivered with each concussion, and his nostrils filled with smoke.

What happened? Where are the girls? He unfastened his seat belt and checked his arms and legs. Everything seemed to work as it should, so he attempted to open his door. The warped mass of metal wouldn't budge. Upon impact, the frame of the driver's side window had crushed like an aluminum can, and only a small hole remained. He had to get out, but he'd never fit through there.

Seeing no other way, he inched closer to the hole, determined to free himself so that he could help his children. Smoke continued to pour from under the crinkled hood, and the temperature inside the vehicle climbed continuously. *Lord God, please help me find Dorothy and Melissa.*

Suddenly, Benard felt hands propelling him from behind up toward the hole and pushing him out of the wreckage. Benard turned to thank his rescuer but saw no one. Puzzled, he scanned the surrounding countryside, and a great sense of awe overcame him. *Thank You, Lord!*

Benard's mind snapped back to his search. "Melissa! Dorothy! Where are you?"

With legs shaking, he hobbled around the car and found blood covering Melissa's small body. The impact had wedged her frame underneath the car seat, and only one small opening held any promise of retrieval. Melissa's bright pink tongue had stiffened and hung out of her mouth like a dead weight. Benard gasped in horror.

"I'm coming, Sweetheart," he called, tears streaming down his cheeks. Groaning and heaving, Benard yanked the seat, but to no avail. He tried again and again, but all strength had left him. Shock overwhelmed him and robbed him of all reason. He must get her out, but how?

"Do not mind, Benard," a voice said. "She is not dead. Please keep pulling, for we are helping you."

Unable to comprehend at the moment, Benard obeyed and pulled Melissa with all his might. Another Power filled his arms and slid down into his legs, enabling him to heave his daughter out of the impossible opening and onto the brown grass beside the car.

Benard stared at Melissa. The school uniform she had proudly adorned this morning now paraded streaks of grease and crimson. He laid a clammy hand on her bloody forehead and prayed. He thought of Dorothy and turned his attention back to the smoldering car, weeping as he called out her name.

"Dorothy, child, where are you?" Nothing. His cries became more frantic. "Dorothy, Dorothy!" *O God, please help me! Where is Dorothy?*

Voices of villagers surrounded him. "She's in the trunk!"

Relief flooded Benard. Several people worked together and extracted her from the wreckage. He stood, paralyzed. *O Lord, let her be all right.* She seemed to be sleeping.

"The car is burning! Hurry, get away from the car!" a voice cried.

Benard tried to force himself into action, but he couldn't seem to move anywhere. Smoke billowed around him and encased the entire scene.

"Hurry! Please come away from there!"

Someone took charge and pulled him to safety with his girls.

"You must get her to a hospital," an older woman said, nodding to Melissa. "Do you have money?"

Benard shook his head. "Not enough." He turned wistful eyes to gaze through tears upon his daughter lying still in the sunset. His heart burned. Remembering how death had stolen his siblings, Benard stood once again on the path to the hospital, wishing he could take Melissa's place. Stroking her matted, bloody hair, he determined to find a way. He eyed the older woman with new courage. "She will go to the best hospital."

The woman nodded with understanding. "Take her to Aga Khan Hospital in Kisumu." She grinned as a private car drew close. "Maybe he will take you!"

Before Benard could comment, she leapt to her feet and ran to the newcomer.

O Lord, please! Benard watched compassion wash over the man's face as she explained the situation. The driver nodded, shifted into park, and hurried to open the door. Moved, Benard fought his desire to weep and gathered Melissa in his arms. Onlookers had already placed Dorothy inside and stepped back so that Benard could lay Melissa next to her sister. He had the presence of mind to utter a brief word of thanks to everyone as he practically fell into the passenger's seat.

The driver respected a comfortable silence the entire way to Kisumu. He never uttered a word, but he did place a gentle hand on Benard's shoulder for a moment and allowed him to see the well of tears in his eyes. Benard gulped.

"Thank you ... thank you for being a good Samaritan to us."

Pamela peered past the white lace curtain, wringing her hands and wishing the matatu would pull into the drive. She wanted to see Melissa, her baby! She shuddered as she recalled the awful night that a pastor in Kisumu had brought Dorothy home to Ahero...

"Excuse me, Mama Pamela?" The man had come to the door alone, not wanting to scare her with Dorothy's appearance.

"Yes?" Pamela's face grew taut.

"I must tell you—there has been an accident." He rushed on as she gasped and put a hand over her mouth. "Please know that everyone is all right."

Her heart sang. *Thank You, Jesus!*

She found her voice. "Where is Benard?"

"He stayed in Kisumu with Melissa." The man peered over Pamela's shoulder into their living quarters. "Perhaps we should sit down," he said in a gentle tone.

Etiquette forgotten, Pamela blushed. "Of course. I'm sorry. Please, feel welcome in our home."

He stepped forward and seated himself on the sofa, focusing on the woman across from him.

"Dorothy is sleeping in my car. She has some minor injuries, but she will heal quickly. Benard has no trouble at all, but Melissa... when I left, she was in the ICU at Aga Khan Hospital." He held up a hand as Pamela started to speak. "She has many wounds, but she will survive. The staff was already making plans to move her to the ward in a day or so."

Benard had called yesterday to inform her of their plans to

come home today, Melissa having spent an entire week in the ward. Pamela had fussed all morning preparing the small room Melissa shared with Dorothy, checking for any hard mattress lumps and mosquito netting holes.

Dorothy peeked around the corner with a smile. "They're here, Mama! They're here!" Dorothy bounded past Pamela and out the front door, waving and giggling all at once.

Sure enough, the open-roofed passenger van rumbled into view as the driver navigated the uneven dung road. Hopefully the ride hadn't caused Melissa too much pain.

Shielding her eyes from the sun, the relieved mother joined Dorothy outside. They returned Benard's waves and Melissa's weak smile with radiant ones of their own.

Pamela tried to hide her concern as she greeted her husband who had flown from the car and into her arms. They embraced and then briefly stared into each others' eyes.

Dorothy had already made her way to Melissa's side, peppering her with questions about her hospital stay. "What was it like? Did they hurt you in there? What did you eat?"

Melissa gave her a wane smile, and Dorothy rushed to hug her. Melissa winced but tried to cover her discomfort.

"Mama, come see Melissa!"

Pamela made her way to Melissa's side and, using great care, drew her daughter close. *O Lord, thank You for being so good to us! Thank You for bringing my girl home.* Crying, Pamela cupped her daughter's face and stroked her shoulder. "You're home, my girl."

In complete exhaustion, Melissa closed her eyes and leaned against her mother.

Benard beamed. "This is the real salvation of the Lord, Pamela."

Dorothy wrapped both of her arms around his waist, and he returned her embrace.

"Our Lord is great and the Victor over death!" Benard's voice boomed. "He has granted us all another day to see His glory again!"

Chapter Twenty-two

Illness

C hills raced up and down his spine. *O Lord, no! Not right now. So many are getting saved!* Invited to speak in a neighboring country, Benard preached the gospel on a platform in front of hundreds of people. Weeping, person after person came forward, desiring to make a commitment to Jesus Christ. *Thank You, Lord, for these precious souls! Please strengthen and sustain me to complete this good work You have started here.*

Beads of sweat popped out all over Benard's body, and alternate waves of hot and cold washed over him. With shaking knees, Benard continued to speak, not in his own strength but with power from a higher Source. "God loves you—won't you let Him be Lord of your life today?"

Benard paused to wipe his face, but the gesture did little good as his hands bore a clammy sheen. Perspiration drenched his clothing from head to toe, and when the chills came, he found them increasingly difficult to bear. He must lie down soon. Still, more people came to the front, and he knew this illness bore all the signs of an enemy attack. *Satan, you will not win. The victory is the Lord's.*

With his jaw set and his adrenaline surging, Benard told no one of his plight and persevered in soul-winning for the final day of his preaching tour. After he had prayed with the last convert, Benard lost all strength.

"Please, I need to go to bed."

One of the event's organizers stared at Benard. "How long have you been ill, Pastor?"

"I . . . I am very sick." Benard mumbled, unable to utter anything else.

His confidant sprang into action, mumbling chastisements to himself for not noticing Benard's poor health earlier. "I thought you looked a little peaked. I should have made you rest this afternoon before tonight's session. Come, Pastor," he ordered as he slipped a supportive arm around Benard's waist. "I will take care of you."

In spite of his pounding headache, Benard tried to think things through. His travel visa for the five-nation African preaching tour expired tomorrow. He didn't know how he would make the trip home. No, with God's strength, he would make it home. To Pamela. He basked in the comfort of the thought. Sweet Pamela. He could not wait to go home.

Thanks to the help of his friend, Benard found himself quickly tucked into the backseat of a small sedan. Within minutes the car bounced over the dung road and stopped suddenly in front of the home where Benard had stayed during his visit. His hostess rushed out and took one look at Benard.

"Malaria." She exchanged glances with the driver. "Pastor Benard, you are very sick. You must rest tonight, and we will see you home tomorrow. Bring him inside."

The driver and another man who had escorted them helped Benard into the small but comfortable home and onto his pallet.

Benard tried to speak. "Th . . . thank . . ."

After mounding a pile of blankets onto the shivering patient, the driver patted him on the arm. "Please, Pastor. Save your strength. You must fight this disease."

The driver spoke to the woman and then turned to Benard. "We will come for you in the morning and pray for you throughout the night." He laid a well-worn hand on Benard's shoulder and beseeched the Lord on Benard's behalf as he drifted off.

"Pamela."

The driver had faithfully delivered Benard home that day. He had gratefully slipped into his own bed while Pamela bustled about making him comfortable. She turned as he spoke her name.

"Th...thank..." Benard relaxed against the pillow in a pool of sweat, exhausted. His skin burned.

Pamela stepped closer and mopped his brow with a cool cloth. After checking to make sure he was comfortable, she stooped and whispered into his ear. "The honor is mine, Benard."

My Pamela, Lord. She is so sick!

For over a week, Pamela had nursed Benard back to health after his intense bout with malaria. Everything seemed to return to normal until Pamela's asthma and lung problems returned.

Please Father, he pleaded as he knelt by her side. She looked so tired. Benard had returned from town discouraged. After e-mailing prayer requests on behalf of his wife to friends all over the world, he had driven home not knowing how to help her. What more could he do?

He struggled not to become angry. Pamela did so much for so many, and here she lay. He wished he could do more to help her. Tears clouded his vision. People could not get the healthcare they needed. His mother now crippled. Betha's new leg problem. Frequent illnesses and fever. Malaria. AIDS. Tuberculosis. Accidents. Elephantitis. Dehydration. Malnutrition. Was there no end? Benard knew that disease accompanied living in a fallen world. Unfortunately, sometimes knowing that didn't make life easier.

Father, please protect us and provide us with medication and treatment. So many are sick and suffering... Let me not become discouraged, Lord. I know You see our pain and hear our cries. You are the Great Physician, and I ask for Your healing hand to be upon my Pamela and upon our people.

Chapter Twenty-three

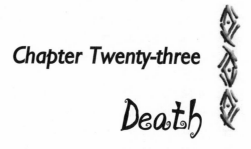

Death

FALL 2005

*F*ather, not the baby. Benard wept long and hard for the sweet baby death had stolen from his dear friend, Pastor Chris. They had looked forward to the coming of this child, enjoyed the baby for a few months, and then... *O God, baby Colby!* Benard cried for the child's father, a faithful partner in their ministry to the street boys.

Their stunned congregation had mourned the loss of baby Colby for days, and today, they would bury the once bubbly, smiley boy. These funerals were the hardest to officiate—the funerals for ones so young. He straightened his tie and headed for the church, praying all the way for God to be with them in the midst of their great sorrow.

"She will not stop crying, Benard," Pamela said, concern showing on her pretty face. "I don't know what to do."

For days, their adopted niece, Christine, had mourned her mother's death compounded by the pain of becoming an orphan. Her father had died tragically two years ago, at which time she had moved in with the Ondieks because her mother wasn't well enough to care for her.

"I will talk to her." Benard eyed his wife and slipped his arm around her waist. "How are you, Pamela? She was your sister..."

Pamela's eyes welled up with tears, and she brushed them away, fiercely trying to hold it together.

"It is very hard, especially since we just buried your niece yesterday and baby Colby last week. So much death . . . no time to fully mourn or recover from loss . . . I will probably cry more, but I will be okay. The Lord is taking care of me."

His heart swelled with love for her. He wished he could ease her pain, take it all away.

Lord, please comfort my sweet Pamela. Give us wisdom in caring for Christine and helping her to live without her mother, as well as the eleven other displaced children we have temporarily taken in as a result of these deaths. Please help them feel loved and wanted, not like a burden to anybody. They are Your children, and we must look after them.

Benard paused. *But how?*

"Good morning, kids. How are you doing today?" Benard stopped in front of a modest cement home with two children playing out front. All smiles, they ran to him for hugs.

"Good morning, Pastor Benard! Won't you play with us?" They held up a muddy little ball, and he could not resist a short game of homemade soccer.

Tattered, dirty shirts clung to their torsos, and their pants frayed at the bottom. Yet, both of these kids seemed oblivious to their poverty and thoroughly enjoyed the fatherly attention they no longer found at home.

Benard teased them without mercy. "Why don't you give me the ball, boy? I will come and take it from you! ROAR!" He lunged toward them, producing giggles and squeals.

Their mother came out and allowed herself a small smile. He hadn't seen her smile since before her husband died last year.

Slap! The ball whacked his left thigh.

"Ouch!" He made a big stink about it. "Who did that to me?"

Both kids ran away looking over their shoulders, intent on escaping yet hoping Benard would chase them.

Finally, out of breath, he handed the ball to their mother.

"Good morning, Sister. Your young ones are feisty today."

She flashed him another small smile and nodded.

"They are good kids, Pastor Benard. Thank you for playing with them. They will talk about it for days."

He saw the pain she tried to hide. "I like your children very much. They are special to me and to God."

Out of the corner of his eye, Benard saw the kids sneaking up. "I think I am getting too old to play. The children are too fast for me."

"No we're not, Pastor Benard," they cried in unison, giving away their position.

"Aha!" Benard snarled and chased them one last time, delighting them. He smiled and tousled the hair of both boys. "I will visit again soon, kids. Take good care of your mama, understand?"

"We will, Pastor Benard. Will you play with us again?" The taller child asked the question, but both waited for his response.

Benard had already begun walking down the road. "Of course I will, " he called over his shoulder, "but you had better practice a lot!"

As he strolled through the Wachara village, Benard mentally reviewed the homes of his beloved family and friends. That one had no husband living in the home, nor that one. Three more over there. He finally concluded that three-quarters of the homes in the village had only women and sometimes children living in them.

Widow. What an awful, lonely word. Benard knew too many widows and wished the Friends of Christ had the funds to feed all of them and their children. Day after day, the women struggled to survive by planting vegetable gardens, selling eggs, and making clothes. Providing for themselves and their children on top of the demanding household chores such as hauling water, chopping firewood, and hand-washing clothes proved difficult, depressing, and exhausting.

Benard walked to his parents' homestead, eager to talk with them. Perhaps there was more they could do for the widows.

But what?

Chapter Twenty-four

Warfare

W e have only this bag of grain left for the month, Pastor Benard."
The schoolteacher pointed to a half-empty flour sack sitting
on the floor. "I don't know what we'll do once it's gone."

All of the orphans lived with relatives or foster families, but often
their only meal of the day consisted of the one bowl of porridge they
received at school.

Benard had no money to feed the orphans this month. What was
he going to do?

He peered into the classroom where dozens of pink and blue
uniformed children clapped their hands and joyfully sang "What a
Mighty God We Serve." A fierce protectiveness rose within him. The
Lord would provide for His little ones. Benard knew He must believe
and trust in Him.

"Thank you for telling me, Mama. I will see what I can do."

She sagged with relief, glad to have shared her burden with
someone. "Thank you, Pastor," she said. "What would we do without
you?"

"It is not I but the Lord who will provide for you and the children, Mama."

She bowed her head. "Thanks be to God."

Hunger
Poverty
Demonic possession
Depression
Few trained pastors
Great suffering
Little money
Illness
Death
Widows
Orphans
Heartache
Dirty water
Grief
Illiteracy
Accidents
Famine
Crime
Starvation
Exhaustion
Hopelessness

Lord, show me how to help Your people!

Part Six

Blessings

A faithful man will be richly blessed.

Proverbs 28:20

Chapter Twenty-five

The Ondiek Household

Benard and Pamela drove eleven-year-old Erick to his mother's house despite his protests. Hopefully, she would take him back into the house.

As they pulled up, Benard thought about many such boys he had accompanied to their homes in order to interview parents or guardians about taking the child back. Benard also interviewed the child to get his side of the story.

During his interview, Erick had insisted that his mother would refuse to take him, but Benard prayed that would not be the case. He must try to reconcile the boy with his mother.

The trio approached the door, and Benard knocked. No answer. He knocked again without receiving a response.

After a moment, the next-door neighbor stepped outside. Her eyes bulged when she saw Erick. "Erick, you're alive!" she exclaimed. "Your mama told me you died."

Erick stared at her. "What?"

Anger darkened the woman's pleasant countenance, and she thrust her hands onto her narrow hips. "Your mama told me she went to your funeral . . ." Her voice broke as the grotesque betrayal reared its ugly head.

Erick swallowed hard and fidgeted with his shirttail. Pamela gasped, and Benard fought tears as he found his voice.

"Do you know where his mama is?"

The neighbor appeared ill.

"She moved awhile ago. She and her twelve children live in an abandoned hotel on the other side of town."

As she gave Benard directions, Pamela guided the boy back to the car. Benard thanked the woman profusely for the information.

She nodded and added one more tidbit. "All of the children have different fathers."

As he began walking away, Benard frowned. He remembered that in America, this practice seemed acceptable somehow, but in Kenya, parenting the children of more than one man was a great taboo. Twelve fathers . . . Benard glanced at the forlorn boy waiting in the car.

Thirteen fathers.

As Pamela's wide eyes took in the rusty tin roof topping the dilapidated hotel, she attempted to distract Erick by talking about the dinner of ugali and thick lentil stew that she planned to cook when he visited on Sunday.

This was the home of thirteen children? It looked like it would collapse any second. Her heart plummeted. *Lord, I cannot send Erick back to this place—I can't. I know we must try to see if his mother will take him, but please, Lord . . .*

Her prayers continued as they met Erick's mother, who asked them what they wanted without even speaking to the boy. She appeared disappointed to see him. As Pamela and Benard entered the dwelling, Erick hung back. Pamela gave silent thanks to God for her husband who put his hand on Erick's shoulder and led him into the house.

Children of all ages and sizes filled the dingy room. Neither they nor the tattered clothes they wore had seen a washtub in months. Some of them had noticed Erick's arrival, but fearful glances at their mother explained why they hadn't waved.

Across the room, four children wrestled with each other while others drew pictures on the walls. Bold cockroaches scurried about the one-room living quarters, deplete of mattresses and the most basic of furnishings. Appalled by the horrid stench and unsanitary conditions, Pamela racked her brain for a positive compliment she could pay her hostess.

Benard motioned her to a seat. Their eyes locked for an instant, and she could sense his apprehension. As she sat, Pamela noticed that Erick and his mother occupied the only other two rickety chairs in the house while Benard remained standing.

Benard began to talk, but Erick's mother held up a hand and turned to face her rambunctious brood. "Get out of here," she yelled to the cow-eyed children staring at the visitors, especially their half-brother. "Play outside, or I'll take a switch to you!"

The kids scattered, and the door slammed behind them.

Dressed in a dirty and faded blue-and-green housedress, the woman yawned, folded her arms, and crossed her legs. "I don't want this boy."

Stunned, Benard and Pamela could not speak. Erick stiffened and became absorbed in fingering the bottom button of his green striped shirt. Righteous anger welled up in Pamela, and tears burned her eyelids. *How dare this woman say such a thing at all, let alone in front of the boy!* Before Pamela realized what she was doing, she leaned forward in her chair and spoke.

"How can you say you don't want him?" Incredulous, she shuddered. "He came from you; you bore him! He is a very good boy. He cleans up after himself—"

"Then you take him. I've got enough to deal with." The woman jutted her jaw toward the playing children and maintained a stubborn, fierce countenance. "Makes no difference to me. One less mouth to feed."

Erick looked as if he wished the floor would swallow him whole.

Benard stepped in. "Mama, he is your child and your responsibility. We found him living on the streets of Kisumu . . ."

Erick's mother leapt to her feet and waved toward the front door. Her eyes flashed, and hatred poured from her lips. "I already told you I don't want this boy. Now get out of my house!"

Without looking back, Erick bolted out the door. Pamela hurried after him while Benard remained inside. Pamela waited for Benard outside in the car where Erick pretended to sleep in the backseat. As she watched Benard walk out of the house toward the car, she noticed that his spirit seemed to have lifted. Her heart filled with hope as Benard swung his lanky frame into the vehicle and shut the door. Leaning toward her, he whispered, "He's coming home with us."

For the first time that morning, Pamela smiled. "I was hoping you'd say that."

Felix waited for Pastor Benard to come. He had said he would be here this afternoon. The thirteen-year-old waited on a street corner wearing his only garments and carrying his few worldly possessions in his pocket. In a desperate act to survive, Felix had come to the street believing life would somehow be better away from his terrible home.

Like a child seeing his first playground, Felix's face lit up as he glimpsed Pastor Benard's tiny white car. *He came! He came for me.* Felix tried to tame his smile. *I knew he wouldn't forget me.*

Waving wildly, Pastor Benard called to him out the open window. "Hello, Felix!"

Pastor Benard had the best face. Felix allowed himself a small wave and stepped toward the car. He couldn't believe this amazing man wanted to take him home to live with him. In Pastor Benard's house! As he neared the vehicle, he saw Mama Pamela's kind smile and a dejected boy in the backseat.

Mama Pamela and Pastor Benard flew out of the car to hug Felix. They both looked happy. Felix twirled around—he couldn't help himself. They wanted him! He tried to comprehend the fact that any adult would want him, much less two at the same time.

"Hi, Mama Pamela! Hi, Pastor Benard!"

"We've come to take you home, Son."

Felix's heart thundered. *Did Pastor Benard just call me Son? Wow!*

Tears came unbidden as his young heart released itself to love these two amazing people.

Thank You, God, Felix prayed. *I believe this day that You are real.*

"We're almost there," Pastor Benard called cheerfully as he pointed to a white house surrounded by a wire fence.

That was his house? Felix gasped. It was huge! A cow and some chickens wandered through the yard, and two children played outside.

"Those are our girls," Pastor Benard announced. "You will meet everyone soon."

Butterflies began to pound against the walls of Felix's stomach. Would the other kids like him? The girls came running to greet them as the car approached. They seemed nice. He glanced at his backseat companion who had not said one word during the entire trip.

"Are you ready, Erick? We get to meet our new family."

Erick said nothing but stared out the window.

Felix tried to ease what he perceived as anxiety. "They want us, Erick. They want us to be a part of their family, not simply stay here. Pastor Benard and Mama Pamela explained it to me." He paused as Erick's head crept sideways until he faced Felix.

"Really?"

"Really." Felix grinned. "We're their sons now."

Erick's head whipped back to the window, and Felix let him retreat into his thoughts. It would probably take awhile for it to sink in for both of them. Felix pondered the miracle the past twenty-four hours had wrought.

Amazing.

As the boys got out of the car, Albert fought the powerful emotions their presence brought to the surface. They looked like he had when he had come to live with the Ondieks. He walked into the living room to meet the newcomers.

"Kids, meet your new brothers, Erick and Felix."

All of the children living with Pastor Benard murmured greetings, and their father introduced them one by one.

"This is Pamela's nephew, Jacob, and her niece, Christine. They came to live with us in 2003."

Christine gave a small, shy wave, and Jacob shook their hands.

"And this is Fred, our houseboy. He tends to the place when we go visiting so that our home can always welcome guests."

Fred flashed the boys a toothy grin, and Albert knew his turn would come next.

"This is Albert, who has just finished Form Four."

The two boys gasped as if they had just met a superhero. Albert grew shy. "I couldn't have done it without our parents."

Pastor Benard placed a hand on Albert's shoulder. "We are very proud of him."

The pastor turned to introduce eight-year-old Melissa and six-year-old Dorothy, but Albert barely heard him. It seemed like just yesterday that while Papa Benard attended CIU, Mama Pamela had come to the shack. He and Ruthie had been so hungry, and Mama Pamela rescued them. She brought food and warm blankets. In the following weeks, not only had Pamela found a home for Albert's young sister with the local school's headmistress, but she had also offered him room and board in exchange for him caring for the Ondiek family livestock.

Albert's eyes glistened with tears as he continued to witness the kindness of these two people. They did so much for others and welcomed people unselfishly into their lives. He tuned back into the family's warm conversation.

"Abraham and Betha are at boarding school, but you will meet them next week when they break for the term. Wycliffe and Sammy, my nephews, will come home then too." Pastor Benard's gaze swept the room. "Did I miss anybody?"

"Pastor Benard?" He turned to find young Felix eager to say something.

"Yes, Son?"

"Thank you for letting us be a part of your family."

Pastor Benard smiled and embraced the boy. He then placed one arm around Erick and the other around Felix drawing them into the family circle. "You belong here, and you will always have a place in our family."

Albert felt his face wet with tears.

Benard checked his watch. Pamela never stayed out this late in the afternoon. She must have taken the girls with her. Typically, when he arrived home from teaching at the seminary or visiting one of the church plants he oversaw, one of his girls ran to greet him and take off his shoes. The ritual proved to create a special bond between himself and his daughters. Today, however, a dark boy slid around the kitchen corner.

"Hello, Papa Benard."

"Hello, Felix." Benard smiled at the boy and lowered himself to the sofa. Before he could bend to pull a shoestring, Felix knelt quietly in front of him. *What was this? A boy would do a girl's job?*

Felix said nothing. The boy had brought a damp rag from the kitchen and carefully began wiping every trace of dung from the red and white treads of Benard's sneakers. First the right, then the left. Benard tried not to stare. After only three days, Felix felt totally at home with Benard to do this. *Thank You, Lord.* The boy finished his task and looked up at Benard.

Benard patted the boy's head. "Well done, Son."

Felix beamed.

After dinner, Mama Pamela made a presentation of clothes Pamela had sewn to Erick and Felix. Benard marveled at her handiwork.

The boys whirled around and held the shirts and pants against their slim bodies. "Thank you, thank you!"

The entire family rejoiced with them in their newfound treasures. All of the kids had seemed to enjoy getting to know each other over the past week. Benard couldn't believe it was only last week. He shook his head, amazed. They had adjusted well. Benard found he could even tease them like he did everyone else. Yesterday, the boys squabbled and jested together, and Benard had joined in the fun.

"I think you boys need some discipline," he said. "Go get a switch."

The boys headed outside and quickly returned. Erick showed his first—a reasonable sized switch sure to do the trick. He stepped aside with a half-smile as Felix revealed the tiny twig he had retrieved. Everyone had belly-laughed as Felix acted out an actual spanking with the scrap of wood.

As he looked around the room at each happy face, Benard's eyes glistened with grateful tears. He caught Pamela's eye, and she smiled at him. She was his perfect complement. She did an amazing job of making the kids feel welcome. She laughed with them and raised them as her own. He sighed with true contentment.

Thank You, Lord, for my precious family.

Chapter Twenty-six

Ongoing Ministry

2006

The click of the phone's off button was deafening in the silent household. Benard must be done. Pamela peered around the corner with a question in her eyes. He looked terrible. Things must not have gone well.

Benard sighed from where he sat on the sofa and motioned her over to sit beside him. "The owner will not budge. The deadline for payment on the five-acre parcel of land is tomorrow."

Slipping her arm around his rigid form, Pamela said nothing as tears flooded her husband's dark cheeks. Poor Benard. He hadn't eaten in three days and was running on only a few hours of sleep. She rubbed his back.

"Pamela, how am I going to tell the people? I put up the fence when we made the original $10,000 payment. If I have to take it down . . . it will be like saying 'God is not powerful enough to do this.'" He wiped his face with the back of his hand. "What will it do to their faith?"

"We must keep praying, Benard," she said. "God has until tomorrow to do a miracle. I believe we should trust Him and ask all of the people to keep praying."

The next morning, Benard awoke, sullen and dejected. Smells of porridge and hot milk filled his nostrils, but he could not eat. The thought nauseated him. He fell to his knees beside the bed, weeping. Some time later, Benard dressed and headed for the living room where Pamela and the children had gathered to pray. He joined them, and they prayed together for the land, the orphans, and a miracle.

The phone rang. Benard leapt to his feet while his family held their breath.

"Hello, Pastor Benard! Greg Wollenhaupt here."

"Pastor Greg, how are you, my friend?"

"I am doing fine, thanks. Pastor Benard, when is the money due on the land?"

"Today."

Pastor Greg cleared his throat, and as he continued speaking, Benard thought he heard a smile in Pastor Greg's voice. *O Lord, could it be...?*

"Well, Pastor Benard, a man just walked into my office and asked if we were still involved with your ministry in Kenya. I filled him in on everything you're doing, and I ended by telling him about the land purchase and deadline."

Benard felt paralyzed. His palms began to sweat, and he looked at Pamela clenching her fists around a towel. *O Lord, what did You do?*

"Pastor Benard, I have a $10,000 check for you in my hand."

"HALLELUJAH!!! PRAISE THE LORD!!!" Benard screamed and leapt around the room. "We have the money! The land is ours!"

Cheers erupted from every corner as children danced and parents gave praise to their mighty God in heaven above.

"Thank You, Lord God! Thank You!"

SEPTEMBER 2008

Benard shook his head. *You continue to amaze me, Lord.* When he least expected it, Benard received encouragement from various financial and spiritual sources. Another ten thousand dollar gift from a North Carolina woman. A construction team bringing both skills and ten thousand dollars. A tractor, more classrooms in Ahero, a new orphanage and church in Wachara. Prayers, financial donations, volunteering missionaries, and food surpluses. *You are so good to us, Father.*

Thank You for Pastor Chris and his help with the street boys and for Alicia. Thank You for Sarah Bothwell and Hungry 4 Him. For Brick-by-Brick, Partners in Evangelism, God's Little Ones, Benard's Vision, Inc. . . . Tears filled his eyes. *You do look after Your children, Father. Thank You.*

In spite of all the ways You have blessed us, our list of needs continues to grow each day. Please keep us in the hearts of our American friends, that they may continue to visit us, pray for us, and give to Your work.

We need them desperately.

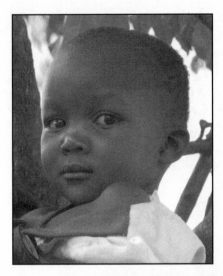

This is the girl Beth Ann Morgan held in her arms and could not feed at the medical clinic in the story. Praise God she survived!

Two dresses made by Mama Pamela worn by Beth Ann Morgan and Pamela Ondiek.

Epilogue

On December 27, 2007, a massive outpouring of rage erupted throughout Pastor Benard's peaceful homeland due to heightened political conflict resulting from the accusation of a rigged presidential election. The people, desperate for change and seeking salvation from the paralyzing oppression, turned to Raila Odinga of the Orange Democratic Party. Praying he would win the presidency and usher out the corrupt regime of President Mwai Kibaki, many hoped to welcome a new government that would right past wrongs.

They were sorely disappointed. A modern-day West Side Story gang war broke out, and bodies piled up in the mortuaries. Because President Kibaki was from the Kikuyu tribe, the largest people-group in Kenya, his opponent's tribe found themselves in grave danger. Raila Odinga hailed from the Luo tribe.

And so did Benard.

Rebels raped the women and set fire to churches with people inside. As the violence escalated, police ordered residents to stay locked inside their homes or be shot.

These standoffs lasted for days at a time, meaning that Benard's 13-member family and the 127 orphans and many widows dependent on him, went for days at a time without food and water.

Risking being shot by poison darts and police bullets, Benard snuck out to find whatever food he could. He passed many houses and churches burned to the ground as well as a pile of about 170 bodies. Through the assistance of a police officer friend and financial donations, Benard purchased enough food and water to get everyone through the crisis.

The political situation has improved overall, but deep healing between the tribes must happen in order for the country to continue moving forward.

As a result of the conflict, many people involved in inter-tribal marriages moved or were violently displaced and cannot be located. AEST lost at least one teacher because of this and for a while struggled to staff its classes.

Benard now reports the Friends of Christ Orphanage in Ahero is doing well with 167 children, many of whom Benard enrolled immediately after the conflict. Thanks to donors and construction team help, three classrooms have been built with plans for more underway.

With another 27 children, Benard and Pamela have started another Friends of Christ Orphanage in Wachara, his home village. And last Sunday morning, 110 adults and children filled the new Wachara church he planted earlier this year. Many are being saved through the testimony of what is happening there.

The future is bright. Talk of daughter churches and agricultural projects has brought the village alive as they work together to improve the lives of their people. The land Benard purchased stands ready for development, and the community is ripe for a hospital, markets, and schools.

Thanks to one selfless, committed couple loving people in practical ways and their great God who faithfully saw them through it all.

A Note from the Author

Join Us

How you can get involved in what God is doing in Kenya

My first exposure to African orphans came while I watched TV and snacked on a peanut butter sandwich after waiting tables during my college years. One of those sponsor-a-child commercials popped across the screen, and after I counted the tips I had earned that evening, I glanced up and saw a big black cauldron.

Pasty-looking porridge had bubbled over one side of the enormous pot which sat over a tiny cooking fire. Within seconds, four scrawny, dirty children leapt onto a rickety platform, peering into the steamy kettle. Their tired, hungry eyes took in the warming food and bulged. Without hesitation, they plunged their bony little hands over the edge and scooped handful after handful into their open mouths as if it were going to disappear before they finished.

I sat mesmerized. I had never seen such raw, unbridled hunger, especially in the desperate faces of children. The peanut butter sandwich stuck in my throat, and my eyes welled with tears.

The commercial ended, and I didn't know what to do. I couldn't eat. I couldn't cry—I was in shock. My tips lay on the table as I tried to wrap my mind around how I could offer unlimited soup, salad, and breadsticks to comfortable customers in a clean, upscale environment while knowing that on this horrible night, children around the world had gone to bed hungry.

Years later while working in a food bank, I had the privilege of not only meeting the nutritional needs of clients but also building relationships with them. God had broken my heart for hungry people, and I decided to go to medical school so that I could become a medical missionary to Africa. That was my plan—not God's.

I developed a heart condition prior to returning to school and within months realized that I would not only have to resign from my current job as a pediatric dietitian but also give up my dream of becoming an overseas missionary. Everything that meant anything was taken away from me—my job, my ability to remember, my healthy body, my income, my ability to drive, my social life, my ministries—everything.

God graciously provided a roof over my head and a family that loved me through those difficult years. He also humbled me and taught me what it means to depend on Him. Gradually, He revealed His plan and purpose for my life—to become a Christian writer, using my gifts, talents, abilities, resources, and influence to speak up for those with no voice and to encourage all who hurt.

I never dreamed the Lord would use me in this way. At times, I balk at having to spend hours alone with my extroverted self and my laptop, but I now realize that as a Christian, my life is not about me. It's about God and what He wants.

I want to obey James 1:27 which says, "Pure and undefiled religion in the sight of our God and Father is this: to visit orphans and widows in their distress, and to keep oneself unstained by the world" (NASB).

This New Testament call to look after orphans seems impossible in light of the limited contact Americans have with orphans, yet it is important because God's Word says so.

Through Pastor Benard and his ministry, God has made a way for all of us to personally connect with not only orphans but also with widows, street children, and impoverished families while carrying out the Great Commission.

I believe this call encompasses the following five dimensions:

1) Prayer

The first thing we can do is pray. Chris Matthews shared during our interview that one of his most cherished memories of his visit to Kenya was waking up each morning while staying in Pastor Benard's home and hearing him pray for every member of the team. Before the sun took its place, this dedicated pastor spent his first minutes of every day asking for God's protection and blessing upon his household and ministry.

His habit sets a challenging example. Ministries like Pastor Benard's face tremendous spiritual attack. Please pray for protection and for the ongoing needs and effectiveness of this ministry. Online updates and specific prayer requests can be found at www.benardsvision.com.

2) Giving

I hesitated to pick up the phone and donate the night I saw the broadcast of the starving children because I didn't know if the organization behind the commercial was credible. I wanted my money to go to hungry African children, not only to meet their physical needs but also their spiritual need for Jesus Christ.

That's why I give a big thank you to the President of Columbia International University, Dr. George Murray, as well as several alumni for endorsing this ministry opportunity. Their passion helps Pastor Benard receive support for the work God is accomplishing in Kenya.

I don't believe in asking people for money. I believe in presenting the opportunity and letting the Holy Spirit move the hearts of the people as He will. If Pastor Benard and Mama Pamela's story has touched you, then I encourage you to act as you will on this unique opportunity to become personally involved in the lives of widows, orphans, and hungry people you have never met. The blessings are tremendous when we give something valuable away, knowing we will never be repaid.

For more information, please visit www.benardsvision.com.

3.) Sponsoring orphans, widows, street children, or students

Would you like to further develop a personal connection in Kenya? Please pray about sponsoring an orphan, widow, street child, or a seminary student with a regular monthly gift. Thanks to the hard work of Sarah Bothwell, many orphans have connected with sponsors, but many children still need sponsors. or more information, I again encourage you to visit www.benardsvision.com or www.hungry4HiM.com.

4.) Telling

Please share with your family and friends about our Kenyan brothers and sisters who need our support. Many ways to help get the word out include, but are not limited to: scheduling a speaking engagement at your church, distributing copies of this book, promoting the Web site, writing an article for a magazine or your local paper. The more exposure we give them, the better.

5.) Going and Serving

One of the highlights of my life was my trip to Kenya. Nothing compares to re-hydrating a wailing infant one dropper-full at a time in a makeshift medical tent in the middle of a wide African plain or worshiping with brothers and sisters in Christ halfway around the world, some who have walked over twenty-five miles to hear teaching from the Word of God.

Many teams have gone, and more are in the works. From construction projects to medical clinics, the needs are wide and varied. The needs have risen dramatically since the announcement of the rigged election in December of 2007. Please consider sharing whatever skills and gifts God has given you with the people of Kenya at www.benardsvision.com.

I pray that together we will be a voice for the orphan and will defend the cause of the widow, the helpless, the impoverished—all those who cannot speak for themselves. Having read the accounts in this book, I trust that you will not walk away unchanged and pray that the Holy Spirit has moved you to get involved and make a difference in peoples' lives, not only in Kenya but also wherever God plants you. May He richly bless you in the coming days—and beyond.

Beth Ann Morgan
December 2008

Friends of Christ Orphanage
in Ahero

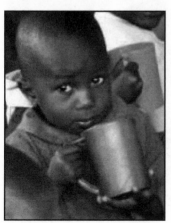

Sarah Bothwell teaching

The New Church in Wachara

Pastor
Benard
preaching
with a melon

Pastor Albert

Friends of Christ Orphanage ~ Wachara

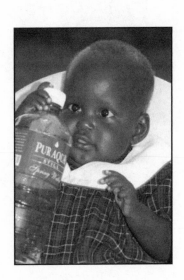

The Staff

Pastor Benard & Mama Pamela

PASTOR BENARD ONDIEK is a man of extraordinary vision dedicated to loving people in practical ways. He is a graduate of Kapsabet Bible College and Columbia International University where he earned his Bachelors Degree and a Masters of Theology respectively. He has planted seven churches, founded a seminary, and started two orphanages. He and his wife, Pamela, reside in Wachara, Kenya, with their eleven children.

To order additional copies of

Benard's Vision:
The Quest of a Kenyan Pastor

please visit
www.BenardsVision.com

The following people are available
to speak about Pastor Benard's ministry
and can be scheduled through
www.benardsvision.com
or at

Beth Ann Morgan
www.themessengerstablet.com

Pastor Greg Wollenhaupt
www.faithefc.com

Sarah Bothwell
www.hungry4HiM.com

Pastor Colby Kinser
www.dublinbiblechurch.org